Quiet
Time

*"The greatest secret of my life
and ministry is my quiet time'*

DAG HEWARD - MILLS

PARCHMENT HOUSE
ACCRA, GHANA AND LONDON, UK

Scripture quotations are taken from the KING JAMES VERSION
of the Bible, unless otherwise stated.

Excerpts from:

*Evidence that demands a Verdict Volume 1 by Josh McDowell
Published by Here's Life Publishers, Inc.,
P.O.Box 1576 San Bernadino, California 92402*

Dakes' Annotated Reference Bible

*The Power of Faith, Article in October 1999 issue of Reader's Digest,
author Phyllis McIntosh.*

All Excerpts Used by Permission

Published by:

Parchment House
P.O. Box 114, Korle-Bu
Accra, Ghana

Parchment House
c/o Lighthouse Chapel International
P.O. Box 3706
London, NW2 1YJ
United Kingdom

ISBN: 9988-596 -93-6

Printed in the EU.

Dedication

I dedicate this book to Mrs. Betty Donkor, my spiritual mother.
Thank you for teaching me how to have my quiet time.

Contents

Quiet Time — Your Personal Time With God

"Quiet Time" is time you spend with God alone. If anybody were to ask me what the greatest secret of my relationship with God is, I would say without any hesitation that it is the power of the quiet times I have with Him everyday. I am eternally grateful to the lady who taught me how to have a quiet time with the Lord every morning. What she taught me has greatly influenced my life to date, and that is why I decided to write this book so that you too can benefit from the power of quiet time.

SEVEN THINGS THAT HAPPEN DURING YOUR QUIET TIME

1.   **During your quiet time you develop the most important relationship of your life.**

A natural relationship develops between any two people who spend quality time together. Spend quality time with God.

Many Christians do not know the importance of this time with God.

2.   **Having a quiet time makes you develop the most important personal habit of all time: a regular time with your Creator.**

I have a quiet time everyday and I spend quality time with the Lord.

3.   **During your quiet time you draw near to God and He draws near to you.**

Draw nigh to God, and he will draw nigh to you. Cleanse your hands, ye sinners; and purify your hearts, ye double minded.

James 4:8

4.   **A quiet time makes you read the most important book in the world.**

The Bible is the most important book in the world. It is the most outstanding volume known to the human race.

Professor M. Montiero-Williams, in comparing other religious books to the Bible said,

[1]*"Pile them, if you will, on the left side of your study table; but place your own Holy Bible on the right side - all by itself, all alone - and with a wide gap between them. For, ...there is a gulf between it and the so-called sacred books of the East which severs the one from the other utterly, hopelessly, and forever ...a veritable gulf which cannot be bridged over by any science of religious thought."*[1]

8

5.   A quiet time is your personal school of the Word.

During your quiet time, you sit and learn at the feet of the Greatest Teacher Jesus left us - the Holy Spirit. He will teach you many things and show you many wonderful revelations in the Word.

> **"I have many things to say unto you, but ye cannot bear them now. Howbeit when he, the Spirit of truth, is come, he will guide you into all truth... and he will shew you things to come"**
>
> John 16:12,13

6.   During your quiet time, you increase in your personal knowledge of the scriptures.

> **..add to your faith virtue; and to virtue knowledge,**
>
> 2 Peter 1:5

> **But grow in grace and in the knowledge of our Lord and Saviour Jesus Christ.**
>
> 2 Peter 3:18

Your personal quiet time gives you the opportunity to add knowledge to your faith.

7.   During your quiet time, you experience the presence of God.

Adam experienced the presence of the Lord in the Garden of Eden until he backslid.

**And they heard the voice of the Lord God walking
in the garden in the cool of the day: and Adam and
his wife hid themselves from the presence of the
Lord God...**

Genesis 3:8

There is a hunger in every man. There is a search in every human being for the presence of God. We all long for the presence of Jehovah. There is nothing like the presence of God. Every preacher longs to feel the presence of God as he ministers. The church service is never the same without the presence of God. Your life will have fullness of joy as you experience the presence of God in your quiet time!

**Thou wilt show me the path of life: in thy presence
is fulness of joy; at thy right hand there are plea-
sures for evermore.**

Psalm 16:11

CHAPTER TWO

Follow The Great Men Who Had Quiet Times

MOSES HAD QUIET TIMES WITH GOD

And the Lord said unto Moses, Hew thee two tables of stone like unto the first: and I will write upon these tables the words that were in the first tables, which thou brakest. AND BE READY IN THE MORNING, AND COME UP IN THE MORNING UNTO MOUNT SINAI, AND PRESENT THYSELF THERE TO ME IN THE TOP OF THE MOUNT. AND NO MAN SHALL COME UP WITH THEE, NEITHER LET ANY MAN BE SEEN THROUGHOUT ALL THE MOUNT; NEITHER LET THE FLOCKS NOR HERDS FEED BEFORE THAT MOUNT. And he hewed two tables of stone like unto the first; and Moses rose up early in the morning, and went up unto mount Sinai, as the Lord had commanded him, and took in his hand the two tables of stone. And the Lord descended in the cloud, and stood with him there, and proclaimed the name of the Lord. And the Lord passed by before him, and proclaimed, The Lord, The Lord God, merciful and gracious, long-suffering, and abundant in goodness and truth, Keeping mercy for thousands, forgiving iniquity and transgression and sin, and that will by no means clear the guilty; visiting the iniquity of the fathers upon the children, and upon the children's children, unto the third and to the fourth genera-tion. And Moses made haste, and bowed his head toward the earth, and worshipped. And he said, If now I have found grace in thy sight, O Lord, let my Lord, I pray thee, go among us; for it is a stiff-necked people; and pardon our iniquity and our sin, and take us for thine inheritance. And he said, Behold, I make a covenant: before all thy people I will do marvels, such as have not been done in all the earth, nor in any nation: and all the people among which thou art shall see the work of the Lord: for it is a terrible thing that I will do with thee.

Exodus 34:1-10

GOD COMMANDED JOSHUA
TO HAVE A DAILY QUIET TIME

This book of the law shall not depart out of thy mouth; but **THOU SHALT MEDITATE THEREIN DAY AND NIGHT**, that thou mayest observe to do according to all that is written therein: for then thou shalt make thy way prosperous, and then thou shalt have good success.

Joshua 1:8

ADAM HAD QUIET TIMES
UNTIL HE BACKSLID

And they heard the voice of the Lord God walking in the garden in the cool of the day: and Adam and his wife hid themselves from the presence of the Lord God amongst the trees of the garden. And the Lord God called unto Adam, and said unto him, Where art thou? And he said, I heard thy voice in the garden, and I was afraid, because I was naked; and I hid myself.

Genesis 3:8-10

PROPHET MICAIAH KNEW
THE HABIT OF QUIET TIME

But Zedekiah the son of Chenaanah went near, and smote Micaiah on the cheek, and said, Which

13

way went the Spirit of the Lord from me to speak unto thee? And Micaiah said, Behold, thou shalt see in that day, when thou shalt go into an inner chamber to hide thyself.

1 Kings 22:24-25

JESUS HAD QUIET TIMES TOO

And in the morning, rising up a GREAT WHILE BEFORE DAY, he went out, and departed into a SOLITARY place, and there prayed.

Mark 1:35

Jesus had His personal quiet time "a great while before day". He also taught His disciples to separate themselves from everybody and spend time alone with God.

But thou, when thou prayest, ENTER INTO THY CLOSET, and when thou hast shut thy door, PRAY TO THY FATHER WHICH IS IN SECRET; and thy Father which seeth in secret shall reward thee openly.

Matthew 6:6

DAVID HAD QUIET TIMES TOO

O God, thou art my God; early will I seek thee: my soul thirsteth for thee, my flesh longeth for thee... When I remember thee upon my bed, and meditate on thee in the night watches.

Psalm 63:1,6

14

CHAPTER THREE

Develop A Strategy For A Successful Quiet Time

THREE STRATEGIES FOR A SUCCESSFUL QUIET TIME

STRATEGY # 1
SET A PRACTICAL, UNCHANGEABLE AND REGULAR TIME FOR YOUR QUIET TIME

Set a regular time when you meet God. It is very important that you set a regular time for your quiet time. Life is such that important things are often overlooked. If you do not schedule a constant period for a quiet time I assure you that you will leave it out. The best time for a quiet time is first thing in the morning.

Notice that Moses had his quiet time in the morning.

And be ready in the MORNING, and COME UP IN THE MORNING unto mount Sinai, and present thyself there to me in the top of the mount. And no man shall come up with thee, neither let any man be seen throughout all the mount; neither let the flocks nor herds feed before that mount.

Exodus 34:2,3

STRATEGY # 2
WITHDRAW FROM THE PRESENCE OF OTHER PEOPLE

And no man shall come up with thee...

Exodus 34:3

A quiet time is not a prayer meeting involving all the members of your household. A quiet time is not another church service or fellowship meeting. It is an intimate time between you and your God. It is a private moment that you must cherish. You will notice that Moses could not have his quiet time in the presence of others. A quiet time is a time when you are alone with God. You cannot develop a personal relationship with someone unless you are alone with the person. It must be possible to withdraw yourself from the company of others so that you can be alone with God.

If you can afford it, you must create for yourself a private place in your home where you go to pray and meet with God.

STRATEGY # 3
CREATE AN ATMOSPHERE THAT IS
CONDUCIVE FOR FELLOWSHIP WITH GOD

You can do this by playing good worship music in the background. If you do not have any such music you can worship the Lord yourself. As you worship the Lord, the presence of the Lord will fill your room. God inhabits praises. There is an atmosphere in which God's presence thrives. I find it easier to pray when I am playing worship music or preaching tapes.

There is no need to struggle in an icy and hardened atmosphere. Put on some music and worship the Lord!

CHAPTER FOUR

Seven Steps To An Effective Quiet Time

STEP #1

PRAY TO BEGIN YOUR QUIET TIME

It's time to give the Lord praise and worship for His goodness. Pray thanking the Lord for another day. Thank Him for who He is, what He has done and what He can and will do. Now ask God to speak to you.

And the Lord passed by before him, and proclaimed, The Lord, The Lord God, merciful and gracious, longsuffering, and abundant in goodness and truth, Keeping mercy for thousands, forgiving iniquity and transgression and sin, and that will by no means clear the guilty; visiting the

iniquity of the fathers upon the children, and upon the children's children, unto the third and to the fourth generation. And Moses made haste, and bowed his head toward the earth, and worshipped.

Exodus 34:6-8

Open thou mine eyes, that I may behold wondrous things out of thy law.

Psalm 119:18

STEP #2

READ A PASSAGE FROM THE BIBLE EXPECTING GOD TO SPEAK TO YOU

Read the passage for the day expecting God to speak to you from it. There are several ways of choosing your daily Bible reading passage.

HOW TO CHOOSE YOUR DAILY BIBLE READING PASSAGE

1. Choose a book of the Bible from which you read a few verses every day. You must always remember where you ended so you can continue from the same place on the next day. In the New Testament, I have had wonderful quiet times as I have read through the books of Luke and Ephesians. In the Old Testament, I have also had wonderful quiet times as I have read through the books of Genesis and 1st and 2nd Samuel.

2. Choose a personality from the Bible whose life story you follow. A few verses from passages about Moses will give you much revelation for your life. You must always remember where you end your reading so that you can start the next day from that point.

3. Take the passage suggested in your daily reading guide. When I first became a Christian, I depended on Our Daily Bread for my quiet time.

STEP #3

MEDITATE (THINK THROUGH AND SOBERLY REFLECT ON WHAT YOU HAVE READ)

If you do not think about what you are reading you will lose a major blessing of the Word of God. Paul told Timothy to think about the Word of God.

> **Consider what I say; and the Lord give thee understanding in all things.**

> 2 Timothy 2:7

SEVEN KEYS TO EFFECTIVE MEDITATION

1. Read the passage slowly.

2. Do not read a very long passage unless it is necessary.

3. Stop at any verse that strikes you and think about it. God's Word is so powerful that only a single word in a verse is enough to change your life. Each quiet time should be a search for that single word that can change your life.

4. Think about the meanings of the words that you are reading.

5. Think about how the scripture applies to life in your generation.

6. **Whisper to the Holy Spirit.** Say, "Help me Holy Spirit to understand your Word. Father, give me the spirit of wisdom and revelation." I have prayed for many years that God should give me the spirit of wisdom and revelation of His Word.

> **That the God of our Lord Jesus Christ, the Father of glory, may give unto you the spirit of wisdom and revelation in the knowledge of him:**
>
> Ephesians 1:17

7. **Decide on a practical way to implement the scriptures that you have learnt.** Without thinking of a way to apply the scripture directly you will often not benefit from your quiet time.

STEP #4

MOVE INTO DEEPER BIBLE STUDY AND MAKE FURTHER REFERENCES TO THINGS THAT STRIKE YOU DURING YOUR QUIET TIME

There are times that you will need to have a longer quiet time. God may minister to you about something. You must be prepared to study further. This is why it is important to have a good reference Bible.

Look through the passage again for as many of the following as possible:

1. What does the passage teach me about the nature of God: the Father, the Son, or the Holy Spirit?

2. Is there a promise for me to believe, and to claim, taking careful note of any conditions attached?

3. Is there a command for me to obey, or a good example for me to follow?

4. Is there a warning for me to heed or a bad example for me to avoid?

5. Is there a prayer for me to pray or remember?

STEP #5

USE YOUR BIBLE READING GUIDE

You may refer to your daily Bible reading guide. These Bible reading guides are very helpful in developing a regular quiet time habit. You will benefit from anointed teachers whose ministry will help you to grow.

STEP #6

WRITE DOWN WHATEVER
THE LORD TELLS YOU

It is important to develop the habit of writing the things that God speaks to you about.

The very fact that you have acquired a notebook shows that you have faith in an invisible God. You believe that He has spoken to you and you have written down His words. You have taken a great step of faith. Without faith it is not possible to please God.

STEP #7

NOW SPEND TIME PRAYING TO THE LORD. LISTEN TO THE VOICE OF THE HOLY SPIRIT

The last step in your quiet time is to pray. At times you will pray for a short time, but there are other times you will pray for a long time. As you have your quiet time regularly, this prayer time will become longer and longer. You will soon desire longer hours with the Lord.

During the prayer time, God will speak to you through His Spirit. There are things God needs to tell you directly through His Spirit. The Holy Spirit is real and you must believe in Him as well.

CHAPTER FIVE

Develop Confidence In The Greatest Book Of All Time!

The Bible is the written Word of God.

> **Knowing this first, that no prophecy of the scripture is of any private interpretation. For the prophecy came not in old time by the will of man: but holy men of God spake as they were moved by the Holy Ghost.**
>
> 2 Peter 1:20,21

SIX THINGS THAT THE
WORD OF GOD IS TO US

1. IT IS A SPECIFIC REVELATION TO MAN.

It reveals the nature of God to man. It explains the origin of man. It gives meaning to man's existence on earth. It reveals the future destiny of all creation. Above all, it reveals God's merciful plan of redemption to us.

Knowing this first, that no prophecy of the scripture is of any private interpretation. For the prophecy came not in old time by the will of man: but holy men of God spake as they were moved by the Holy Ghost.

2 Peter 1:20,21

God, who at sundry times and in divers manners spake in time past unto the fathers by the prophets, Hath in these last days spoken unto us by his Son, whom he hath appointed heir of all things, by whom also he made the worlds;

Hebrews 1:1,2

2. IT IS THE GOSPEL OF SALVATION FOR MANKIND.

The gospel is the good news of Christ's saving power for us. The Bible is the only book that shows how man can be saved.

For I am not ashamed of the gospel of Christ: for it is the power of God unto salvation to every one

that believeth; to the Jew first, and also to the Greek.

Romans 1:16

3. IT IS AUTHORITATIVE AND FINAL.

The Bible is not a discussion of ideas and theories. It is an authoritative declaration of the facts. The truths that are expounded are awesome and non-negotiable. The aura surrounding the Bible is partly due to its authoritative and irrevocable truths.

Therefore we ought to give the more earnest heed to the things which we have heard, lest at any time we should let them slip. For if the word spoken by angels was stedfast, and every transgression and disobedience received a just recompense of reward; How shall we escape, if we neglect so great salvation; which at the first began to be spoken by the Lord, andwas confirmed unto us by them that heard him; God also bearing them witness, both with signs and wonders, and with divers miracles, and gifts of the Holy Ghost, according to his own will?

Hebrews 2:1-4

4. THE WORD OF GOD IS INSPIRED DIVINELY.

This is what differentiates the Bible from every other book. The Bible claims to have inspiration and motivation from God. In other words, it was virtually written by God through the hands of mortal men.

All scripture is given by inspiration of God, and is profitable for doctrine, for reproof, for correction, for instruction in righteousness:

2 Timothy 3:16

5. THE WORD OF GOD IS POWERFUL AND SEARCHING.

How true this is! Thousands of people are converted when the simple truths of the Bible are shared. I was changed by the Word of God when I encountered it.

For the word of God is quick, and powerful, and sharper than any twoedged sword, piercing even to the dividing asunder of soul and spirit, and of the joints and marrow, and is a discerner of the thoughts and intents of the heart.

Hebrews 4:12

6. THE WORD OF GOD IS GOD'S METHOD FOR MAN'S PROSPERITY AND ABUNDANT LIFE.

God's method for prosperity is not by clever ideas and human tricks. It is through His Word.

This book of the law shall not depart out of thy mouth; but thou shalt meditate therein day and night, that thou mayest observe to do according to all that is written therein: for then thou shalt make thy way prosperous, and then thou shalt have good success.

Joshua 1:8

My son, attend to my words; incline thine ear unto my sayings. Let them not depart from thine eyes; keep them in the midst of thine heart. For they are life unto those that find them, and health to all their flesh.

Proverbs 4:20-22

SIX THINGS THAT THE BIBLE IS

²**1. The Bible is God's inspired revelation of the original destiny of all things.** Here heaven is opened, and the gates of Hell disclosed. It is the traveller's map, the pilgrim's staff, the pilot's compass, the soldier's sword, and the Christian's charter.

2. The Bible is the power of God unto eternal salvation and the source of present help, for body, soul, and spirit. (Romans 1:16; John 15:7). Christ is its grand subject, man's good its design, and the glory of God its end. It is a mine of wealth, the source of health, and a world of pleasure.

3. The Bible is God's will or testament to men in all ages, revealing the plan of God for man here and now, and in the next life. It will be opened at the judgement; and it will last forever. It involves the highest responsibility; will reward for the least to the greatest of labour; and will condemn all who trifle with its sacred contents.

4. The Bible is the record of God's dealings with man in the past, present and future. It contains His message of eternal salvation for all who believe in Christ, and eternal damnation for all who rebel against the gospel.

5. As a literary composition, the Bible is the most remarkable book ever written. It is a divine library of 66 books some of considerable size, and others no larger than a tract. These books include various forms of literature - history, biography, poetry, proverbial sayings, hymns, letters, directions for elaborate ritualistic worship, laws, parables, riddles, allegories, prophecy, and all other forms of human expression.

6. The Bible is the only book that reveals the mind of God, the state of man, the way of salvation, the doom of sinners, and the happiness of believers. Its doctrines are holy, its precepts binding, its histories true and its decisions immutable. It contains light to direct, spiritual food to sustain, and comfort to cheer. Man should read it to be wise, believe it to be safe, and practice it to be holy; he should read it that it might fill his memory, rule his heart, and guide his feet in righteousness and true holiness. He should read it slowly, frequently, prayerfully, meditatively, searchingly, devotionally; and study it constantly, perseveringly and industriously through and through - until it becomes a part of his being, generating faith that will move mountains.[2]

EIGHT THINGS THAT THE BIBLE IS NOT

[3]**1. The Bible is not an amulet, a charm, a fetish, or anything to work wonders by its very presence alone.** It does not claim to be such; it does claim that if one will study and practice its teachings he will see wonders worked in his life both now and in the hereafter.

2. The Bible is not a book of chronological events or an unbroken series of divine utterances. It was given, here a little and there a little, to many men through eighteen centuries (Isaiah 28:9-11): but regardless of this it, forms a perfect unity.

3. The Bible is not a book of heavenly utterances in supernatural languages; it is God's revelation in the simplest human language possible.

4. The Bible is not a book of mysteries; it explains its so-called mysteries, and is so self-interpreting that no mystery remains.

5. The Bible is not a book that says one thing and means another. Generally, the passages have one simple meaning. In the few, which have a double meaning this fact, is quite clear, either from the verses themselves or from parallel passages. One cannot, as is sometimes said get a thousand different meanings from the scriptures.

6. The Bible is not a specimen of God's skill as a writer or logician. It is a book written by men who He used to record His revelation. The method was by giving them ways of expressing truth, and freedom in the use of their own language. What inspiration guarantees is unity of truth, not sameness of words and expressions.

7. The Bible is not a book of systematic discourses on any one subject; but it does give divine information on practically every subject. One must collect together from here and there, all God's information through various writers, in order to know the whole truth. When this is done there is perfect harmony, and everything, which a man really needs to know about a subject, is clear.

8. The Bible is not a book adapted to the tastes, customs and habits of any one nation or people; it is not for any one age or period of time. It is a book for which all people in all ages can conform and yet retain their own lawful customs and habits, which are not contrary to the will of God.[3]

CHAPTER SIX

The Origin Of The Bible

Ye shall not add unto the word which I command you, neither shall ye diminish ought from it, that ye may keep the commandments of the Lord your God which I command you.

Deuteronomy 4:2

THE CANON

Many so-called inspired writers claimed to be inspired of God. There were many letters and books that were available to God's people. There was therefore the need to define the officially accepted writings of inspired men. These officially accepted books and writings are what are known as the Canon of scripture.

The Canon means "the body of sacred writings that are accepted as genuine and inspired." The Old Testament Canon is the list of Old Testament books and the New Testament Canon is the final accepted list of New Testament books and writings.

An important truth you must not overlook is that the Church did not create the Canon or the books that we call scripture. The Church simply recognized the books that were inspired by God and publicly approved of them.

Notice what F.F. Bruce said:

4*When at last a church council - the Synod of Hippo in AD 393 listed the twenty-seven books of the New Testament, it did not confer upon them any authority which they did not already possess, but simply recorded their previously established canonicity. (The ruling of the Synod of Hippo was re-promulgated four years later by the Third Synod of Carthage.) Since that time, there has been no serious questioning of the twenty-seven accepted books of the New Testament by Roman Catholics or Protestants.*4

5*As far as the Old Testament is concerned, the Christian Church and the Jews share the same Canon of scripture. Although the Christian Church has the same Old Testament Canon, the number of books differs because:*

i.   The Christian Church divides the books of Samuel, Kings and Chronicles into two books each.

ii. The Jews consider the minor Prophets as one book whereas the Christians consider them separately.

iii. The order of the books in the Christian Bible is different from the order in the Jewish law.

Here is a breakdown of the Jewish Old Testament Canon which is divided into the Law (Torah), The Prophets (Nebhim) and The Writings (Kethubhim).

Section 1: The Law (Torah)	Section 2: The Prophets (Nebhim)	Section 3: The Writings (Kethubim)
Genesis Exodus Leviticus Numbers Deuteronomy	A. Former Prophets Joshua Judges Samuel Kings B. Latter Prophets Isaiah Jeremiah Ezekiel The Twelve	A. Poetical Books Psalms Proverbs Job B. Five Rolls Song of Songs Ruth Lamentations Esther Ecclesiastes C. Historical Books Daniel Ezra - Nehemiah Chronicles [5]

FIVE REASONS WHY THE CANON OF SCRIPTURE WAS DEFINED

[6]*1. The Jewish people established their Canon of scripture, which we call the Old Testament. Christians accept this Old Testament Canon primarily because Jesus accepted it.*

The Jewish sacrificial system was ended by the destruction of Jerusalem and the temple in 70 AD. Even though the Old Testament Canon was settled in the Jewish mind long before 70 AD, there was a need for something more definitive. The Jews were scattered and they needed to determine which books were the authoritative Word of God because of the many extra scriptural writings and the decentralization. The Jews became a people of one book and it was this book that kept them together.

2. *Christianity started to blossom and many writings of the Christians were beginning to be circulated.* The Jews needed to expose these Christian writings vividly and exclude them from their writings and their use in the synagogues.[6]

[7]**3. *The New Testament Canon became necessary because of the emergence of heretics.*** Heretics were people who held opinions and practiced things which were contrary to accepted beliefs. For instance, Marcion 140 AD developed his own Canon and began to propagate it. The church needed to offset his influence by determining what the real Canon of New Testament scripture was.

4. *Many eastern churches were using books in services that were definitely incorrect.* It called for a decision concerning the Canon.

5. *The Edict of Diocletian 303 AD, declared the destruction of the sacred books of the Christians.* Who wanted to die for just a religious book? They needed to know! [7]

TWENTY REASONS WHY SOME WRITINGS WERE INCLUDED OR EXCLUDED FROM THE BIBLE

When a writing is not part of the Bible it is called a non-canonical writing. The more well known rejected writings are the books of the Apocrypha as well as other writings. They are not accepted as canonical and therefore have been excluded from the Bible. What was the basis for their inclusion or exclusion from the Bible? Were they just haphazardly thrown in or were there very sound reasons for their inclusion in the Bible?

Below are several reasons why some of the writings were accepted or rejected for inclusion in the Bible.

> **Knowing this first, that no prophecy of the scripture is of any private interpretation. For the prophecy came not in old time by the will of man: but holy men of God spake as they were moved by the Holy Ghost.**
>
> 2 Peter 1:20,21

[8]*1. Many books and writings were accepted because Jesus Christ accepted them and quoted from them*[8]. Our Lord's endorsement of these books is more than enough to justify the inclusion of these writings as holy scripture. In the upper room Jesus told the disciples *"that all things must be fulfilled, which were written in the law of Moses, and the Prophets, and the Psalms concerning Me."* (Luke 24:44) With these words "He indicated the three sections into which the Hebrew Bible was divided - the

Law, the Prophets, and the 'Writings' (here called 'the Psalms'
probably because the Book of Psalms is the first and longest
book in this third section)."[8]

**And he said unto them, These are the words
which I spake unto you, while I was yet with you,
that all things must be fulfilled, which were written in the law of Moses, and in the prophets, and
in the psalms, concerning me.**

Luke 24:44

[9] *Jesus disagreed with the oral traditions of the Pharisees (Mark 7,
Matthew 15), not with their concept of the Hebrew Canon. "There is
no evidence whatever of any dispute between Him and the Jews as to
the canonicity of any Old Testament book."*[9]

**Then the Jews took up stones again to stone him.
Jesus answered them, Many good works have I
showed you from my Father; for which of those
works do ye stone me? The Jews answered him,
saying, For a good work we stone thee not; but
for blasphemy; and because that thou, being a
man, makest thyself God. Jesus answered them,
Is it not written in your law, I said, Ye are gods? If
he called them gods, unto whom the word of God
came, and the scripture cannot be broken; Say ye
of him, whom the Father hath sanctified, and sent
into the world, Thou blasphemest; because I said,
I am the Son of God?**

John 10:31-36

From the blood of Abel unto the blood of Zacharias, which perished between the altar and the temple: verily I say unto you, It shall be required of this generation.

Luke 11:51

That upon you may come all the righteous blood shed upon the earth, from the blood of righteous Abel unto the blood of Zacharias son of Barachias, whom ye slew between the temple and the altar.

Matthew 23:35

10 "...from the blood of Abel to the blood of Zechariah." Jesus here confirms His witness to the extent of the Old Testament canon. Abel, as everyone knows, was the first martyr (Genesis 4:8). Zechariah is the last martyr to be named (in the Hebrew Old Testament order. Having been stoned while prophesying to the people "in the court of the house of the Lord! (2 Chronicles 24:21). Genesis was the first book in the Hebrew canon and Chronicles the last book. Jesus basically said "from Genesis to Chronicles," or, according to our order, "from Genesis to Malachi." 10

11 *2. Some of the books were accepted because they were authoritative.* Some books were not authoritative and were believed not to have come from the hand of God.

3. When a book was not written by a holy man of God or a prophet, it was rejected. The scripture says that holy men of God spoke the words of prophecy as they were moved by the

39

Holy Spirit. We cannot accept books and writings that do not come from holy men of God who were moved by the Holy Spirit.

4. Writings were accepted because they were authentic, genuine and original. The Church Fathers had the policy of "if in doubt, throw it out!" This enhanced the validity of their discernment of canonical books.

5. Some writings were accepted because they were powerful and dynamic. Writings that did not come with the life transforming power of God were not included.

6. Books that were received, collected, read and used by the people of God were accepted. The Apostle Peter recognized, received and used the writings of Paul as scripture. (2 Peter 3:16). The fact that Peter recognized the writings of Paul gave credence to the letters of Paul.[11]

[12] **7. Books that were excluded from the Jewish Canonical scripture were rejected.** Such books were therefore excluded from the Christian Old Testament. You will notice that the Christian Old Testament is the same as the Jewish Torah (The Law), Nebhim (The Prophets) and Kethubhim (The Writings).

8. Jesus and the New Testament writers never once quoted from the Apocrypha and other unacceptable writings. However, there are hundreds of quotes and references to almost all of the canonical books of the Old Testament. This is a fact that is even more striking when we realize that Paul, who even quoted twice from heathen poets, did not quote from the Apocrypha.[12]

[13] *9. The last Old Testament prophet predicted that the next messenger coming to Israel from God would be the forerunner of Christ*[13] (Malachi 3:1). Most of the apocryphal books were written during the period of Malachi and Christ. These apocryphal writers were not the forerunners of Christ and therefore were not considered as significant enough for inclusion.

10. Divine authority is not claimed by the apocryphal authors; and by others it is virtually disowned. [13]

> **These five books of Jason I shall try to summarize in a single work; for I was struck by the mass of statistics and the difficulty which the bulk of the material causes to those wishing to grasp the narratives of this history.**
>
> 2 Maccabees 2:23,24 (The New English Bible)

> **At this point I will bring my work to an end. If it is found well written and aptly composed, that is what I myself hoped for; if cheap and mediocre, I could only do my best.**
>
> 2 Maccabees 15:38 (The New English Bible)

[14] *11. Some of the writings were rejected because they were at variance with Bible history.* Such inaccuracies were not acceptable in the Bible.

12. Some unacceptable writings, as well as the Apocrypha, are self-contradictory and in some cases opposed to doctrines of scripture.

13. *The Apocryphal books were not a part of the ancient versions of the scripture.* They were first added after 300 AD. The Laodicean Council in 363 AD rejected them as being uninspired, thus proving that by that time some were claiming inspiration from them.

14. *The Apocrypha is unacceptable because even the Roman Catholic Church did not accept it as canonical for 1,546 years.* One wonders why they included the Apocrypha after so many years.

15. *Jewish historians did not regard the Apocrypha as scripture.* Josephus (AD 30-100), a Jewish historian, explicitly excludes the Apocrypha, numbering the books of the Old Testament as 22.

16. *Jewish philosophers did not regard the Apocrypha as scripture.* Philo (20 BC - AD 40), an Alexandrian Jewish Philosopher, quoted the Old Testament prolifically and even recognized the threefold division, but he never quoted from the Apocrypha as inspired.

17. *For the first four centuries after the death of Christ, no canon or council of the Christian church recognized the Apocrypha as inspired.*

18. *Many of the fathers of the early church spoke out against the Apocrypha; for example Origen, Cyril of Jerusalem, Athanasius.*

19. *Jerome (340-420 AD), the great scholar and translator of the Vulgate (4th Century Latin Version of the Bible), rejected the Apocrypha as part of the canon.* He disputed across the

Mediterranean with Augustine on this point. He at first refused even to translate the Apocryphal books into Latin, but later he made a hurried translation of a few of them. After his death, and literally "over his dead body," the Apocryphal books were brought into his Latin Vulgate directly from the Old Latin Version.

20. Many of the Reformers and even Roman Catholic scholars through the Reformation period rejected the Apocrypha.

Martin Luther and the reformers rejected the canonicity of the Apocrypha.[14]

CHAPTER SEVEN

You Don't Need The Aprocrypha, Stay With The Bible!

Apocrypha comes from the Greek word, 'apokruphos' meaning 'hidden or concealed'. The Apocrypha consists of the books added to the Old Testament that are not considered canonical by Protestants.

FOUR REASONS WHY THE APOCRYPHA IS NOT CANONICAL

[15] *1. The Apocrypha abounds in historical and geographical inaccuracies and anachronisms.*

2. The Apocrypha teaches doctrines which are false and fosters practices which are at variance with inspired scripture.

3. The Apocrypha resorts to literary types and displays artificiality of subject matter and styling which is out of keeping with inspired scripture.

4. The Apocrypha lacks distinctive elements which give genuine scripture their divine character, such as prophetic power and poetic and religious feeling. [15]

Most Christians do not know what the Apocrypha is and what it contains so I have decided to include a short summary of its individual books.

A SUMMARY OF THE APOCRYPHA

[16] 1 ESDRAS (150 BC)

This book tells about the restoration of the Jews to Palestine after the Babylonian exile. It draws considerably from Chronicles, Ezra and Nehemiah, but the author has added much legendary material. The most interesting item is the story of the three guardsmen. They were debating what was the strongest thing in the world. One said, "Wine." Another, "The king." The third, "Woman and truth." They put these three answers under the king's pillow. When he awoke he required the three men to defend their answers. The unanimous decision was: truth is greatly and supremely strong. Because Zerubabel had given this answer he was allowed to rebuild the temple at Jerusalem.

2 ESDRAS (AD 100)

It is an apocalyptic work, containing seven visions. Martin Luther was so confused by these visions that he is said to have thrown the book into the Elbe River.

TOBIT (EARLY 2ND CENTURY BC)

This book is a short novel. Strongly Pharisaic in tone, it emphasizes the Law, clean foods, ceremonial washings, charity, fasting and prayer. It is clearly unscriptural in its statement that almsgiving atones for sin.

JUDITH (ABOUT THE MIDDLE OF 2ND CENTURY BC)

This is also fictitious and Pharisaic. The heroine of this novel is Judith, a beautiful Jewish widow. When her city was besieged she took her maid, together with Jewish clean food, and went out to the tent of the attacking general. He was enamored of her beauty and gave her a place in his tent. Fortunately, he had imbibed too freely and sank into a drunken stupor. Judith took his sword and cut off his head. Then she and her maid left the camp, taking his head in their provision bag. It was hung on the wall of a nearby city and the leaderless Assyrian army was defeated.

ADDITIONS TO ESTHER (ABOUT 100 BC)

Esther stands alone among the books of the Old Testament in having no mention of God. We are told that Esther and Mordecai fasted but not specifically that they prayed. To compensate for this lack, the additions have long prayers attributed to these two, together with a couple of letters supposedly written by Artaxerxes.

THE WISDOM OF SOLOMON (ABOUT AD 40)

This book was written to keep the Jews from falling into scepticism, materialism, and idolatry. As in Proverbs, Wisdom is personified. There are many noble sentiments expressed in this book.

ECCLESIASTICUS, OR WISDOM OF SIRACH (ABOUT 180 BC)

This apocryphal book shows a high level of religious wisdom, somewhat like the canonical Book of Proverbs. It also contains much practical advice. For instance, on the subject of after-dinner speeches it says (32:8):

"Speak concisely; say much in few words..."

"Act like a man who knows more than he says."

And again (33:4):

"Prepare what you have to say, and then you will be listened to."

In his sermons John Wesley quotes several times from the Book of Ecclesiasticus. It is still widely used in Anglican circles.

BARUCH (ABOUT AD 100)

This book represents itself as being written by Baruch, the scribe of Jeremiah, in 582 BC. Actually, it is probably trying to interpret the destruction of Jerusalem in AD 70. The book urges the Jews not to revolt again, but to be in submission to the emperor. In spite of this the Bar-Cochba revolution against Roman rule took place soon after, in AD 132-135. The sixth chapter of Baruch contains the so-called "Letter of Jeremiah," with its strong warning against idolatry - probably addressed to Jews in Alexandria, Egypt.

Our Book of Daniel contains 12 chapters. In the first century before Christ a thirteenth chapter was added, the story of Susanna. She was the beautiful wife of a leading Jew in Babylon, to whose house the Jewish elders and judges frequently came. Two of these became enamored of her and tried to seduce her. When she cried out, the two elders said they had found her in the arms of a young man. She was brought to trial. Since there were two witnesses who agreed in their testimony, she was convicted and sentenced to death.

But a young man named Daniel interrupted the proceedings and began to cross-examine the witnesses. He asked each one separately under which tree in the garden they had found Susanna with a lover. When they gave different answers they were put to death and Susanna was saved.

Bel and the Dragon was added at about the same time and called chapter 14 of Daniel. Its main purpose was to show the folly of idolatry. It really contains two stories.

In the first, King Cyrus asked Daniel why he did not worship Bel, since that deity showed his greatness by daily consuming many sheep, together with much flour and oil. So Daniel scattered ashes on the floor of the Temple where the food had been placed that evening. In the morning the king took Daniel in to show him that Bel had eaten all the food during the night. But Daniel showed the king in the ashes on the floor the footprints of the priests and their families who had entered secretly under the table. The priests were slain and the temple destroyed.

The story of the Dragon is just as obviously legendary in character. Along with Tobit, Judith, and Susanna, these stories may be classified as purely Jewish fiction. They have little if any religious value.

The Song of the Three Hebrew Children follows Daniel 3:23 in the Septuagint and the Vulgate. Borrowing heavily from Psalm 136 and Psalm 148, it is antiphonal like Psalms 136, having 32 times the refrain: "Sing praise to him and greatly exalt him forever."

THE PRAYER OF MANASSEH WAS COMPOSED IN MACCABEAN TIMES (2ND CENTURY BC)

This was composed in Maccahean times as the supposed prayer of Manasseh, the wicked king of Judah. It was obviously suggested by the statement in 2 Chronicles 33:19 - "His prayer also, and how God was entreated of him... behold, they are written among the sayings of the seers." Since this prayer is not found in the Bible, some scribe had to make up the deficiency!

1 MACCABEES (1ST CENTURY BC)

This is perhaps the most valuable book in the Apocrypha. It describes the exploits of the three Maccabean brothers - Judas, Jonathan, and Simon. Along with Josephus it is our most important source for the history of this crucial and exciting period in Jewish history.

2 MACCABEES (SAME TIME)

Is not a sequel to 1 Maccabees, but a parallel account, treating only the victories of Judas Maccabeus. It is generally thought to be more legendary than 1 Maccabees.[16]

CHAPTER EIGHT

Appreciate The Greatness Of The Word Of God

4 REASONS WHY THE BIBLE CAN BE TRUSTED

1. THE BIBLE CAN BE TRUSTED BECAUSE PROMISES MADE GENERATIONS EARLIER HAVE BEEN KEPT.

Blessed be the Lord, that hath given rest unto his people Israel, according to all that he promised: there hath not failed one word of all his good promise, which he promised by the hand of Moses his servant.

1 Kings 8:56

2. THE BIBLE CAN BE TRUSTED BECAUSE GOD STANDS
BY HIS WORD UNTIL IT COMES TO PASS.

For I am the Lord: I will speak, and the word that I shall speak shall come to pass; it shall be no more prolonged: for in your days, O rebellious house, will I say the word, and will perform it, saith the Lord God.

Ezekiel 12:25

For verily I say unto you, Till heaven and earth pass, one jot or one tittle shall in no wise pass from the law, till all be fulfilled.

Matthew 5:18

Then said the LORD unto me, Thou hast well seen: for I will hasten my word to perform it.

Jeremiah 1:12

3. THE BIBLE CAN BE TRUSTED BECAUSE IT
IS UNCHANGING IN A CHANGING WORLD.

But the word of the Lord endureth for ever. And this is the word which by the gospel is preached unto you.

1 Peter 1:25

4. HEAVEN AND EARTH WILL PASS AWAY BUT THE
WORD OF GOD WILL REMAIN FOREVER.

Heaven and earth shall pass away, but my words shall not pass away.

Matthew 24:35

Heaven and earth shall pass away: but my words shall not pass away.

Luke 21:33

CHAPTER NINE

Why The Bible Is Superior To Every Other Book

Most people do not understand the uniqueness and superiority of this great book. It is a book like no other book. If someone asks you for the meaning of the word 'unique', you might as well say it means "Bible". Unique in the dictionary is defined as: 'the one and only. It also means: to be different from all others, having no like or equal'.

TWENTY-NINE REASONS WHY THE BIBLE IS SUPERIOR TO EVERY OTHER BOOK ON EARTH

1. The Bible is superior in the fact that it is the most reliable historic document of all time. When we do not have the original historical document, we must establish how reliable the copies are. This is done in two ways:

i.   The more identical manuscript copies of the original we have, the more sure we are that the copies reflect what is in the original document.

ii.   The shorter the time interval between the copy and the original, the more sure we are that the copy reflects what is in the original.

[17] "There are more than 5,300 known Greek manuscripts of the New Testament. Add over 10,000 Latin Vulgate and at least 9,300 other early versions (MSS) and we have more than 24,000 manuscripts copies of portions of the New Testament in existence today."

"No other document of antiquity even begins to approach such numbers and attestation. In comparison, the book Iliad by Homer is second with only 643 manuscripts that still survive. The first complete preserved text of Homer dates from the 13th century."[17]

[18] *John Warwick Montgomery says* that "to be sceptical of the resultant text of the New Testament books is to allow all of classical antiquity to slip into obscurity, for no documents of the ancient period are as well attested bibliographically as the New Testament."[18]

[19] *Sir Frederic G. Kenyon*, who was the director and principal librarian of the British Museum and second to

none in authority for issuing statements about MSS, says, "...besides number, the manuscripts of the New Testament differ from those of the classical authors, and this time the difference is clear gain. In no other case is the interval of time between the composition of the book and the date of the earliest extant manuscripts so short as in that of the New Testament. The books of the New Testament were written in the latter part of the first century; the earliest extant manuscripts (trifling scraps excepted) are of the fourth century - say from 250 to 300 years later."

"This may sound a considerable interval, but it is nothing to that which parts most of the great classical authors from their earliest manuscripts. We believe that we have in all essentials an accurate text of the seven extant plays of Sophocles; yet the earliest substantial manuscript upon which it is based was written more than 1400 years after the poet's death."

Kenyon continues in The Bible and Archaeology: "The interval then between the dates of original composition and the earliest extant evidence becomes so small as to be in fact negligible, and the last foundation for any doubt that the scriptures have come down to us substantially as they were written has now been removed. Both the authenticity and the general integrity of the books of the New Testament may be regarded as finally established." [19]

2. The Bible is superior to other books because archaeology has constantly confirmed its historical accuracy and validity.

[20] *"Nelson Glueck, the renowned Jewish archaeologist, wrote:* "It may be stated categorically that no archaeological discovery has ever controverted a biblical reference." He continued his assertion of "the almost incredibly accurate historical memory of the Bible, and particularly so when it is fortified by archaeological fact."

William F. Albright, known for his reputation as one of the great archaeologists, states: "There can be no doubt that archaeology has confirmed the substantial historicity of Old Testament tradition."

Albright adds: "The excessive scepticism shown toward the Bible by important historical schools of the eighteenth and nineteenth centuries, certain phases of which still appear periodically, has been progressively discredited. Discovery after discovery has established the accuracy of innumerable details, and has brought increased recognition to the value of the Bible as a source of history." [20]

3. The Bible is superior in its unity and continuity.
Over forty authors wrote sixty-six books over a period of 1,500 years. Many never saw the writings of the others and yet there is no contradiction between any two of them. Collect any group of books of any other forty men on any subject and see if they agree.

NINE FACTS ABOUT THE UNITY
AND CONTINUITY OF THE BIBLE

[21] *a. The Bible was written over a 1,500 years span.*

b. The Bible was written over 40 generations.

c. The Bible was written by over 40 authors from every walk of life:
- § Moses, a political leader, trained in the universities of Egypt
- § Peter, a fisherman
- § Amos, a herdsman
- § Joshua, a military general
- § Nehemiah, a cupbearer
- § Daniel, a prime minister
- § Luke, a doctor
- § Solomon, a king
- § Matthew, a tax collector
- § Paul, a rabbi

d. The Bible was written in different places:
- § Moses in the wilderness
- § Jeremiah in a dungeon
- § Daniel on a hillside and in a palace
- § Paul, inside prison walls
- § Luke, while travelling
- § John, on the isle of Patmos
- § Others in the rigors of a military campaign.

e. The Bible was written at different times:
- § David in times of war
- § Solomon in times of peace

f. The Bible was written during different moods:
   § Some writing from the heights of joy and others
      writing from depths of sorrow and despair.
g. The Bible was written on three continents:
   § Asia, Africa and Europe

h. The Bible was written in three languages:
   § Hebrew: The language of the Old Testament.
      It was called "the language of Judah" in
      2 Kings 18:26-28
      and in Isaiah 19:18, "the language of Canaan".
   § Aramaic: This was the "common language" of the
      Near East until the time of   Alexander the Great
      (6th century BC - 4th century BC).
   § Greek: The New Testament language. This was
      the international language at the time of Christ.

i. The Bible includes in its subject matter hundreds of controversial subjects. A controversial subject is one, which creates opposing opinions when mentioned or discussed. Biblical authors spoke on hundreds of controversial subjects with harmony and continuity from Genesis to Revelation.

*The result is one unfolding story: "**God's redemption of man!**"*

WHAT F.F. BRUCE SAID ABOUT THE BIBLE

"Any part of the human body can only be properly explained in reference to the whole body. And any part of the Bible can only be properly explained in reference to the whole Bible."

"The Bible, at first sight, appears to be a collection of literature - mainly Jewish. If we inquire into the circumstance under which the various

Biblical documents were written, we find that they were written at intervals over a space of nearly 1400 years."

"The writers wrote in various lands, from Italy in the west to Mesopotamia and possibly Persia in the east."

"The writers themselves were a heterogeneous number of people, not only separated from each other by hundreds of years and hundreds of miles, but also belonging to the most diverse walks of life. In their ranks we have kings, herdsmen, soldiers, legislators, fishermen, statesmen, courtiers, priests and prophets, a tent-making Rabbi and a Gentile physician, not to speak of others of whom we know nothing apart from the writings they have left us."

"The writings themselves belong to a great variety of literary types. They include history, law (civil, criminal, ethical, ritual, and sanitary), religious poetry, didactic treatises, lyric poetry, parable and allegory, biography, personal correspondence, personal memoirs and diaries."[21]

[22] **4. The Bible is more distinctive than every other book ever published.** The Bible is superior to other books in its origin, formation, doctrines, principles, claims, moral tone, histories, prophecies, revelation, literature, present redemption and eternal benefits.

5. Unlike other books published, the Bible has a vast influence in this world. The Bible has blessed millions of people of every generation. The Bible has contributed to the creation of the greatest civilizations on earth. It has given man the highest hope and destiny.

6. The wisest most godly and honest men in this world acknowledge the Bible as the Word of God. Only infidels and ungodly people reject the Bible.

7. Unlike many other books, the Bible was written by honest and godly men. This is because it condemns all sin and records the sins and faults of its writers as well as others. This is something evil men would not do. Even good men would not do this unless they were inspired to do so to help others.

8. The Bible meets all the needs of mankind. All man's present and eternal needs are met by the Bible.

9. The Bible has been preserved through the ages. Whole kingdoms and religions have sought in vain to destroy it. God has made the Bible indestructible and victorious.

10. The Bible is superior to other books because the heavenly and eternal character of its contents prove it to be of God.

11. The preaching of the Bible changes the lives of people. The response of humanity to this great book shows that it is of a supernatural and superior nature.

12. The Bible is superior in its infinite depths and lofty ideals.

13. The Bible stands out in supremacy by the unbelievable number of prophecies that it contains. About three thousand three hundred prophecies have been fulfilled. Predictions made hundreds and even thousands of years earlier have been fulfilled. Not one detail has failed yet. About 2,908 verses are being fulfilled or will be fulfilled.

14. The Bible is superior in its miraculous nature. Hundreds of miracles are recorded in the scriptures. Miracles happen daily among those who pray and claim Bible promises.

15. The Bible is alone in its flawlessness. The Bible is scientifically and historically correct. No one man has found the Bible at fault in any of its many hundreds of statements of history, astronomy, botany, geology, geography or any other branch of learning.

16. The Bible is superior in its adaptability. The Bible is always up to date on every subject. It can be applied to the lives of people who live in Africa, Asia, Europe or America. It was useful to people who lived a thousand years ago and it is still relevant to the people who live in the twenty first century.

17. The Bible is superior in its moral and spiritual power. It meets perfectly every spiritual and moral need of man.

18. The Bible is superior in its doctrines. The doctrines of the Bible surpass all human ideas or principles of relationships, religion and culture.

19. The Bible is superior because it claims to be the Word of God. Bible writers claimed that God spoke what they wrote. In other words, the Bible itself claims to be the Word of God.

20. The Bible is superior in secular history. Many pagan, Jewish and Christian writers confirm the facts of the Bible. They actually quote the Bible as being genuine, authentic and inspired of God.

21. The Bible is superior in its worldwide circulation. Most authors have their books circulated within communities. You will be surprised to find that many authors who are very popular are not known at all in other parts of the world. Not so with the Bible! [22]

[23] "The Bible has been read by more people and published in more languages than any other book. There have been more copies produced of its entirety and more portions and selections than any other book in history. Some will argue that in a designated month or year more of a certain book was sold. However, over all there is absolutely no book that reaches or even begins to compare to the circulation of the Scriptures."

WHAT HY PICKERING SAID ABOUT THE BIBLE

Hy Pickering said that about 30 years ago, for the British and Foreign Bible Society to meet its demands, it had to publish:

> One copy every three seconds day and night, 22 copies every minute day and night, 1,369 copies every hour day and night, 32,876 copies every day in the year.

> It is deeply interesting to know that this amazing number of Bibles was dispatched to various parts of the world in 4,583 cases weighing 490 tons! [23]

22. The Bible is superior in its worldwide translations.

[24] The Bible was one of the first major books translated (Septuagint: Greek translation of the Hebrew Old Testament, ca 250 BC). It has been translated and retranslated and paraphrased more than any other book in existence.

Encyclopaedia Britannica says "by 1966 the whole Bible had appeared... in 240 languages and dialects... one or more whole books of the Bible and 739 additional ones, a total publication of 1,280 languages."

Three thousand Bible translators between 1950-1960 were at work translating the Scriptures.

The Bible factually stands unique ("one of a kind; alone in its class") in its translation.[24]

23. The Bible is superior in its continued existence through the years.

[25] Being written on material that perishes, having to be copied and recopied for hundreds of years before the invention of the printing press, did not diminish its style, correctness or existence. The Bible, compared with other ancient writings, has more manuscript evidence than any 10 pieces of classical literature combined.

WHAT JOHN WARWICK MONTGOMERY SAID ABOUT THE BIBLE

"To be sceptical of the resultant text of the New Testament books is to allow all of classical antiquity to slip into obscurity, for no documents of the ancient period are as well attested bibliographically as the New Testament."

WHAT JOHN LEA SAID ABOUT THE BIBLE

John Lea in ' The Greatest Book in the World, compared the Bible with Shakespeare's writings. He had this to say:

"It seems strange that the text of Shakespeare, which has been in existence less than two hundred and eight years, should be far more uncertain and corrupt than that of the New Testament, now over eighteen centuries old, during nearly fifteen of which it existed only in manuscript.

...With perhaps a dozen or twenty exceptions, the text of every verse in the New Testament may be said to be so far settled by general consent of scholars, that any dispute as to its readings must relate rather to the interpretation of the words than to any doubts respecting the words themselves. But in everyone of Shakespeare's thirty seven plays there are probably a hundred readings still in dispute, a large portion of which materially affects the meaning of the passages in which they occur."[25]

24. The Bible is superior in its ability to survive persecution.

WHAT SIDNEY COLLETT SAID ABOUT THE BIBLE

[26] *Voltaire, the noted French infidel who died in 1778, said that in one hundred years from his time Christianity would be swept from existence and passed into history. But what has happened? Voltaire has passed into history, while the circulation of the Bible continues to increase in almost all parts of the world, carrying blessing wherever it goes.*

Concerning the boast of Voltaire on the extinction of Christianity and the Bible in 100 years, Geisler and Nix point out that "only fifty years after his death the Geneva Bible Society used his press and house to produce stacks of Bibles." What an irony of history?

In AD 303, Diocletian issued an edict (Cambridge History of the Bible, Cambridge University Press, 1963) to stop Christians from worshipping and to destroy their Scriptures.

"...An imperial letter was everywhere promulgated, ordering the razing of the churches to the ground and the destruction by fire of the Scriptures, and proclaiming that those who held high positions would lose all civil rights while those in households, if they persisted in the profession of Christianity, would be deprived of their liberty."

The historic irony of the above edict to destroy the Bible is that Eusebius records the edict given 25 years later by Constantine, the emperor following Diocletian, that 50 copies of the Scriptures should be prepared at the expense of the government.[26]

25. The Bible is superior in its ability to endure criticism.

WHAT H.L. HASTINGS SAID ABOUT THE BIBLE

[27] H.L. Hastings has forcibly illustrated the unique way the Bible has withstood the attacks of infidels and sceptics.

"Infidels for eighteen hundred years have been refuting and overthrowing this book, and yet it stands today as solid as a rock. Its circulation increases, and it is more loved and cherished and read today than ever before.

Infidels, with all their assaults, make about as much impression on this book as a man with a tack hammer would on the Pyramids of Egypt.

When the French monarch proposed the persecution of the Christians in his dominion, an old statesman and warrior said to him, "Sire, the church of God is an anvil that has worn out many hammers." So the hammers of infidels have been pecking away at this book for ages, but the hammers are worn out, and the anvil still endures.

If this book had not been the book of God, men would have destroyed it long ago. Emperors and popes, kings and priests, princes and rulers have all tried their hand at it; they die and the book still lives."

WHAT BERNARD RAMM SAID ABOUT THE BIBLE

"A thousand times over, the death knell of the Bible has been sounded, the funeral procession formed, the inscription cut on the tombstone, and committal read. But somehow the corpse never stays put.

No other book has been so chopped, knifed, sifted, scrutinized, and vilified. What book on philosophy or religion or psychology or belles letters of classical or modern times has been the subject to such a mass attack as the Bible? With such venom and scepticism? With such thoroughness and erudition? Upon every chapter, line and tenet?

The Bible is still loved by millions, read by millions, and studied by millions."[27]

26. The Bible is superior in the nature of its prophecies.

[28] Wilbur Smith who compiled a personal library of 25,000 volumes writes:

"It is the only volume ever produced by man, or a group of men in which is to be found a large body of prophecies relating to individual nations, to Israel, to all the peoples of the earth, to certain cities, and to the coming of One who was to be the Messiah; The ancient world had

many different devices for determining the future, known as divination, but not in the entire gamut of Greek and Latin literature, even though they use the words prophet and prophecy, can we find any real specific prophecy of a great historic event to come in the distant future, nor any prophecy of a Saviour to arise in the human race.

"Mohammedanism cannot point to any prophecies of the coming of Mohammed uttered hundreds of years before his birth. Neither can the founders of any cult in this country rightly identify any ancient text specifically foretelling their appearance."[28]

27. The Bible is superior in its honesty.

The Bible deals very frankly with the sins of its characters. Read the biographies today, and see how they try to cover up, overlook or ignore the shady side of people. Take the great literary geniuses; most are painted as saints. The Bible does not do it that way. It simply tells it like it is.

28. The Bible is superior in its influence on surrounding literature.

WHAT CLELAND B. MCAFEE SAID ABOUT THE BIBLE

Cleland B. McAfee writes in The Greatest English Classic:

[29]*"If every Bible in any considerable city were destroyed, the Book could be restored in all its essential parts from the quotations on the shelves of the city public library. There are works, covering almost all the great literary writers, devoted especially to showing how much the Bible has influenced them."*

WHAT KENNETH SCOTT LATOURETTE
SAID ABOUT JESUS

Kenneth Scott Latourette, former Yale historian, says:

"It is evidence of His importance, of the effect that He has had upon history and presumably, of the baffling mystery of His being that no other life ever lived on this planet has evoked so huge a volume of literature among so many peoples and languages, and that, far from ebbing, the flood continues to mount."

A professor once remarked: "If you are an intelligent person, you will read the one book that has drawn more attention than any other, if you are searching for the truth!"

29. The Bible is superior because it has set unusual records.

i.   The Bible is the first religious book to be taken into outer space.

ii.   It is also one of the (if not the) most expensive books.

        Gutenberg's Latin Vulgate Bible sold for over $100,000.The Russians sold the Codex Sinaiticus (an early copy of the Bible) to England for $510,000.

iii.   The longest telegram in the world was the Revised Standard Version of the New Testament sent from New York to Chicago[29].

CHAPTER TEN

Your Quiet Time Will Reveal the Total Message of the Bible

As you have your quiet time regularly, God will show you the overall messages that He has for mankind. These messages can be gleaned from the Bible. There are eight major themes that run through the entire Bible.

1. THE NATURE OF GOD

A. HE IS A CREATOR

And God said, Let us make man in our image, after our likeness: and let them have dominion over the fish of the sea, and over the fowl of the air, and over the cattle, and over all the earth, and

over every creeping thing that creepeth upon the earth. So God created man in his own image, in the image of God created he him; male and female created he them. And God blessed them, and God said unto them, Be fruitful, and multiply, and replenish the earth, and subdue it: and have dominion over the fish of the sea, and over the fowl of the air, and over every living thing that moveth upon the earth. And God said, Behold, I have given you every herb bearing seed, which is upon the face of all the earth, and every tree, in the which is the fruit of a tree yielding seed; to you it shall be for meat. And to every beast of the earth, and to every fowl of the air, and to every thing that creepeth upon the earth, wherein there is life, I have given every green herb for meat: and it was so.

Genesis 1:26-30

B. HE PROVIDES FOR OUR NEEDS

But my God shall supply all your need according to his riches in glory by Christ Jesus.

Philippians 4:19

He that spared not his own Son, but delivered him up for us all, how shall he not with him also freely give us all things?

Romans 8:32

C. GOD IS HOLY

In the year that king Uzziah died I saw also the Lord sitting upon a throne, high and lifted up, and his train filled the temple. Above it stood the seraphims: each one had six wings; with twain he covered his face, and with twain he covered his feet, and with twain he did fly. And one cried unto another, and said, Holy, holy, holy, is the Lord of hosts: the whole earth is full of his glory. And the posts of the door moved at the voice of him that cried, and the house was filled with smoke. Then said I, Woe is me! for I am undone; because I am a man of unclean lips, and I dwell in the midst of a people of unclean lips: for mine eyes have seen the King, the Lord of hosts. Then flew one of the seraphims unto me, having a live coal in his hand, which he had taken with the tongs from off the altar: And he laid it upon my mouth, and said, Lo, this hath touched thy lips; and thine iniquity is taken away, and thy sin purged.

Isaiah 6:1-7

But as he which hath called you is holy, so be ye holy in all manner of conversation; Because it is written, Be ye holy; for I am holy.

1 Peter 1:15,16

D. GOD IS LOVING

He that loveth not knoweth not God; for God is love. In this was manifested the love of God

73

toward us, because that God sent his only begotten Son into the world, that we might live through him. Herein is love, not that we loved God, but that he loved us, and sent his Son to be the propitiation for our sins.

1 John 4:8-10

E. GOD IS JUST AND HAS TWO SIDES: HIS GOODNESS AND HIS SEVERITY

Behold therefore the GOODNESS AND SEVERITY OF GOD: on them which fell, severity; but toward thee, goodness, if thou continue in his goodness: otherwise thou also shalt be cut off.

Romans 11:22

2. THE CREATION AND THE ORIGIN OF MAN

A. GOD IS THE CREATOR OF HEAVEN AND EARTH

In the beginning God created the heaven and the earth. And the earth was without form, and void; and darkness was upon the face of the deep. And the Spirit of God moved upon the face of the waters.

Genesis 1:1,2

For by him were all things created, that are in heaven, and that are in earth, visible and invisible, whether they be thrones, or dominions, or principalities, or powers: all things were created by

him, and for him: And he is before all things, and by him all things consist.

Colossians 1:16,17

B. GOD CREATED THE UNIVERSE BY SPEAKING IT INTO EXISTENCE

Through faith we understand that the worlds were framed by the word of God, so that things which are seen were not made of things which do appear.

Hebrews 11:3

C. GOD IS THE GIVER OF LIFE

The thief cometh not, but for to steal, and to kill, and to destroy: I am come that they might have life, and that they might have it more abundantly.

John 10:10

D. MAN IS CREATED IN GOD'S IMAGE

And God said, Let us make man in our image, after   our likeness...

Genesis 1:26

E. MAN WAS GIVEN DOMINION OVER EARTH

... and let them have dominion over the fish of the sea, and over the fowl of the air, and over the cattle, and over all the earth...

Genesis 1:26

3. THE FALL OF MAN AND THE CONSEQUENCES OF THE FALL

A. MAN WAS TEMPTED AND FELL INTO SIN

And the Lord God said unto the woman, What is this that thou hast done? And the woman said, The serpent beguiled me, and I did eat. And the Lord God said unto the serpent, Because thou hast done this, thou art cursed above all cattle, and above every beast of the field; upon thy belly shalt thou go, and dust shalt thou eat all the days of thy life: And I will put enmity between thee and the woman, and between thy seed and her seed; it shall bruise thy head, and thou shalt bruise his heel. Unto the woman he said, I will greatly multiply thy sorrow and thy conception; in sorrow thou shalt bring forth children; and thy desire shall be to thy husband, and he shall rule over thee. And unto Adam he said, Because thou hast hearkened unto the voice of thy wife, and hast eaten of the tree, of which I commanded thee, saying, Thou shalt not eat of it: cursed is the ground for thy sake; in sorrow shalt thou eat of it all the days of thy life; Thorns also and thistles shall it bring forth to thee; and thou shalt eat the herb of the field; In the sweat of thy face shalt thou eat bread, till thou return unto the ground; for out of it wast thou taken: for dust thou art, and unto dust shalt thou return.

Genesis 3:13-19

B. Sin entered into the world and through sin death came

For if by one man's offence death reigned by one; much more they which receive abundance of grace and of the gift of righteousness shall reign in life by one, Jesus Christ.) Therefore as by the offence of one judgment came upon all men to condemnation; even so by the righteousness of one the free gift came upon all men unto justification of life.

Romans 5:17,18

C. The life of men became shorter and shorter as sin increased

For the wages of sin is death; but the gift of God is eternal life through Jesus Christ our Lord.

Romans 6:23

4. GOD'S CHOICE AND DEALINGS WITH THE NATION OF ISRAEL - A TYPE OF THE CHURCH

A. GOD CHOSE ABRAHAM, ISAAC AND JACOB

Now the Lord had said unto ABRAM, Get thee out of thy country, and from thy kindred, and from thy father's house, unto a land that I will show thee: And I will make of thee a great nation, and I will bless thee, and make thy name great; and thou shalt be a blessing: And I will bless them that bless thee, and curse him that curseth thee: and in thee shall all families of the earth be blessed.

Genesis 12:1-3

And God said, Sarah thy wife shall bear thee a son indeed; and thou shalt call his name Isaac: and I will establish my covenant with him for an everlasting covenant, and with his seed after him. And as for Ishmael, I have heard thee: Behold, I have blessed him, and will make him fruitful, and will multiply him exceedingly; twelve princes shall he beget, and I will make him a great nation. But my covenant will I establish with ISAAC, which Sarah shall bear unto thee at this set time in the next year.

Genesis 17:19-21

And JACOB went out from Beersheba, and went toward Haran. And he lighted upon a certain place, and tarried there all night, because the sun was set; and he took of the stones of that place, and put them for his pillows, and lay down in that place to sleep. And he dreamed, and behold a ladder set up on the earth, and the top of it reached to heaven: and behold the angels of God ascending and descending on it. And, behold, the Lord stood above it, and said, I am the Lord God of Abraham thy father, and the God of Isaac: the land whereon thou liest, to thee will I give it, and

to thy seed; And thy seed shall be as the dust of the earth, and thou shalt spread abroad to the west, and to the east, and to the north, and to the south: and in thee and in thy seed shall all the families of the earth be blessed. And, behold, I am with thee, and will keep thee in all places whither thou goest, and will bring thee again into this land; for I will not leave thee, until I have done that which I have spoken to thee of.

Genesis 28:10-15

B. GOD USED JOSEPH TO DELIVER ISRAEL FROM STARVATION AND FAMINE

C. GOD USED MOSES TO DELIVER HIS PEOPLE FROM BONDAGE AND TEACH THEM HIS LAWS

D. GOD'S PEOPLE ISRAEL, LIKE THE CHURCH, KEPT GOING ASTRAY TO SERVE OTHER GODS

Now will I sing to my wellbeloved a song of my beloved touching his vineyard. My wellbeloved hath a vineyard in a very fruitful hill: And he fenced it, and gathered out the stones thereof, and planted it with the choicest vine, and built a tower in the midst of it, and also made a winepress therein: and he looked that it should bring forth grapes, and it brought forth wild grapes. And now, O inhabitants of Jerusalem, and men of Judah, judge, I pray you, betwixt me and my vineyard. What could have been done more to my

vineyard, that I have not done in it? wherefore, when I looked that it should bring forth grapes, brought it forth wild grapes? And now go to; I will tell you what I will do to my vineyard: I will take away the hedge thereof, and it shall be eaten up; and break down the wall thereof, and it shall be trodden down: And I will lay it waste: it shall not be pruned, nor digged; but there shall come up briers and thorns: I will also command the clouds that they rain no rain upon it. For the vineyard of the Lord of hosts is the house of Israel, and the men of Judah his pleasant plant: and he looked for judgment, but behold oppression; for righteousness, but behold a cry.

Isaiah 5:1-7

5. GOD'S MASTER PLAN OF SALVATION THROUGH JESUS CHRIST

...There is none righteous, no, not one:

Romans 3:10

For all have sinned, and come short of the glory of God;

Romans 3:23

For the wages of sin is death...

Romans 6:23

For God so loved the world, that he gave his only begotten Son, that whosoever believeth in him

should not perish, but have everlasting life. For God sent not his Son into the world to condemn the world; but that the world through him might be saved.

John 3:16,17

He came unto his own, and his own received him not. But as many as received him, to them gave he power to become the sons of God...

John 1:11, 12

Christians are released into a new life of blessings in Christ Jesus.

Blessed be the God and Father of our Lord Jesus Christ, who hath blessed us with all spiritual blessings in heavenly places in Christ: According as he hath chosen us in him before the foundation of the world, that we should be holy and without blame before him in love: Having predestinated us unto the adoption of children by Jesus Christ to himself, according to the good pleasure of his will, To the praise of the glory of his grace, wherein he hath made us accepted in the beloved. In whom we have redemption through his blood, the forgiveness of sins, according to the riches of his grace; Wherein he hath abounded toward us in all wisdom and prudence; Having made known unto us the mystery of his will, according to his good pleasure which he hath purposed in him-

self: That in the dispensation of the fulness of times he might gather together in one all things in Christ, both which are in heaven, and which are on earth; even in him: In whom also we have obtained an inheritance, being predestinated according to the purpose of him who worketh all things after the counsel of his own will: That we should be to the praise of his glory, who first trusted in Christ. In whom ye also trusted, after that ye heard the word of truth, the gospel of your salvation: in whom also after that ye believed, ye were sealed with that holy Spirit of promise, Which is the earnest of our inheritance until the redemption of the purchased possession, unto the praise of his glory.

Ephesians 1:3-14

According as his divine power hath given unto us all things that pertain unto life and godliness, through the knowledge of him that hath called us to glory and virtue: Whereby are given unto us exceeding great and precious promises: that by these ye might be partakers of the divine nature, having escaped the corruption that is in the world through lust.

2 Peter 1:3,4

6. THE RELEASE OF GOD'S ARMY
- THE BUILDING OF THE CHURCH

A. CHRIST WILL BUILD A CHURCH, AN ARMY
OF BELIEVERS WHO WILL WIN THE LOST AT ANY COST

And I say also unto thee, That thou art Peter, and upon this rock I will build my church; and the gates of hell shall not prevail against it.

Matthew 16:18

B. CHRIST GIVES ALL BELIEVERS A DUTY TO GO
INTO THE WHOLE WORLD AND PREACH THE GOSPEL

Go ye therefore, and teach all nations, baptizing them in the name of the Father, and of the Son, and of the Holy Ghost: Teaching them to observe all things whatsoever I have commanded you: and, lo, I am with you alway, even unto the end of the world. Amen.

Matthew 28:19,20

But ye shall receive power, after that the Holy Ghost is come upon you: and ye shall be witnesses unto me both in Jerusalem, and in all Judaea, and in Samaria, and unto the uttermost part of the earth.

Acts 1:8

C. EVERY SINGLE BELIEVER IS A MEMBER OF THE ARMY
AND IS CREATED SPECIALLY TO DO GOOD WORKS FOR THE LORD

For we are his workmanship, created in Christ

Jesus unto good works, which God hath before ordained that we should walk in them.

Ephesians 2:10

D. THE CHURCH IS FEARLESS, POWERFUL, ANOINTED AND FULL OF GOD'S AUTHORITY

Verily, verily, I say unto you, He that believeth on me, the works that I do shall he do also; and greater works than these shall he do; because I go unto my Father.

John 14:12

7. THE ETERNAL JUDGEMENT OF NATIONS, SINNERS AND CHRISTIANS

A. GOD WILL JUDGE ALL NATIONS.
JESUS SPOKE OF THE JUDGEMENT OF THE NATIONS

And before him shall be gathered all nations: and he shall separate them one from another, as a shepherd divideth his sheep from the goats: And he shall set the sheep on his right hand, but the goats on the left. Then shall the King say unto them on his right hand, Come, ye blessed of my Father, inherit the kingdom prepared for you from the foundation of the world:

Matthew 25:32-34

B. GOD WILL JUDGE ALL CHRISTIANS

For we must all appear before the judgment seat of Christ; that every one may receive the things

84

done in his body, according to that he hath done, whether it be good or bad.

2 Corinthians 5:10

c. GOD WILL JUDGE ALL SINNERS

And I saw a great white throne, and him that sat on it, from whose face the earth and the heaven fled away; and there was found no place for them.

Revelation 20:11

8. THE ETERNAL FUTURE: A NEW HEAVEN AND EARTH

And I saw a new heaven and a new earth: for the first heaven and the first earth were passed away; and there was no more sea.

Revelation 21:1

CHAPTER ELEVEN

Tap Into The Hidden Power Of Quiet Time

The reason why many people do not have a quiet time is because they do not know the effect it has on them.

FIFTEEN POWERFUL EFFECTS OF A DAILY QUIET TIME

1. A DAILY QUIET TIME PREVENTS HURTS AND REDUCES PAIN IN THIS LIFE.

Much of the pain and hurts of this life would have been avoided if we had used the light of life.

Then spake Jesus again unto them, saying, I am the light of the world: he that followeth me shall not walk in darkness, but shall have the light of life.

John 8:12

When a man gropes about in darkness he often hurts himself by bumping into unexpected or unforeseen objects. How painful it is to hit your shin against a table. The pains and hurts we experience in our lives are because we have not picked up the lamp of God.

Thy word is a lamp unto my feet, and a light unto my path.

Psalm 119:105

There will I make the horn of David to bud: I have ordained a lamp for mine anointed.

Psalm 132:17

What is this lamp that God has specially prepared for His anointed ones? It is the Word of God!

The sorrows that some have experienced in marriage have come because they did not use the lamp of God to guide them into marriage. Many people pick up the lamp of God after they have been severely injured by the experiences of life. A lamp is not intended to soothe your pain but to prevent you from getting hurt. How much better a life we would have if we would pick up this lamp on a daily basis. The lamp will keep us from the pain and injuries.

It is only a quiet time that can provide you with constant illumination. If you live in darkness from Monday to Saturday and only receive a little light on Sunday, surely your life will not be the same as someone who lives in constant illumination. Do you want constant illumination for your life? Begin to have a regular quiet time!

You will reduce the sorrow of your life by using the true light that God has ordained for you. It is the only light which can light the way for every man on this earth.

That was the true Light, which lighteth every man that cometh into the world.

John 1:9

2. A DAILY QUIET TIME GUARANTEES A GOOD HARVEST OF NICE THINGS.

This is because a daily quiet time is the sowing of spiritual seeds into your spirit. The Word of God is the great seed that you plant in your heart when you have a quiet time.

Now the parable is this: The seed is the word of God.

Luke 8:11

Being born again, not of corruptible seed, but of incorruptible, by the word of God, which liveth and abideth for ever.

1 Peter 1:23

Every time you have a quiet time you are making an investment into your life. You sow the seed of the Word of God and it will yield the fruit of love, peace and joy in the Holy Spirit. Have you wondered why there is little or no love, peace and joy in your life? These fruits can only come as you sow a spiritual seed into your life.

For he that soweth to his flesh shall of the flesh reap corruption; but he that soweth to the Spirit shall of the Spirit reap life everlasting.

Galatians 6:8

Most Christians sow into the flesh. They invest in their flesh. They invest time, money to the development of their flesh and their earthly existence. Others invest seeds of television, pleasure, sex, alcohol and drugs into their flesh. The harvests that come from such seeds are horrific.

Most pastors are pastoring sheep who live under the devastating effects of a massive harvest from the flesh. It is our duty as pastors to lead the sheep to invest in their spirits on a daily basis.

3. A DAILY QUIET TIME BURNS AWAY UNWANTED THINGS.

When this fire is received on a daily basis, no evil can remain as part of your character.

Wherefore thus saith the Lord God of hosts, Because ye speak this word, behold, I will make my words in thy mouth fire, and this people wood, and it shall devour them.

Jeremiah 5:14

Some things can only be removed by fire. The Word of God **is like fire**. A daily dose of that fire will take care of every unwanted element in your personality or character.

4. A DAILY QUIET TIME BREAKS DOWN EVIL STRONGHOLDS.

90

Because a quiet time leads to the breaking and the burning of evil things in our lives, Christians who do not have quiet times often have bad character. The strongholds in most Christians' lives cannot be broken away by one powerful sermon. Anyone who does not have a regular quiet time has a lot of things that need to be burnt and broken down.

Is not my word like as a fire? saith the Lord; and like a hammer that breaketh the rock in pieces?

Jeremiah 23:29

5. A DAILY QUIET TIME LEADS TO THE CUTTING AWAY OF UNWANTED ASPECTS OF OUR LIVES AND CHARACTER.

Once again you will see that Christians who just listen to sermons on Sundays but have no regular cutting away of evil tendencies are very different people from those who have a regular quiet time.

For the word of God is quick, and powerful, and sharper than any twoedged sword, piercing even to the dividing asunder of soul and spirit, and of the joints and marrow, and is a discerner of the thoughts and intents of the heart.

Hebrews 4:12

6. A REGULAR QUIET TIME PUTS A WEAPON INTO THE HAND OF THE BELIEVER.

Satan has a good laugh at Christians who are unarmed and exposed. The daily act, which Satan hates, and fears is when you arm yourself daily with the sword of the Spirit. Prayer is good. Fasting is good. Going to church is good. But none of these can replace the daily arming of God's soldier.

The Word of God has a way of slipping out of our hands. This is because of the pressures of the world in which we live. The opinions of unbelievers, sinners, worldly Christians have a way of eroding the effect of the Word of God on our lives. This is why it is necessary to regularly place the sword into our hands so that we will be ready for every trick of the devil.

And take the helmet of salvation, and the sword of the Spirit, which is the word of God:

Ephesians 6:17

7. QUIET TIMES DELIVER CHRISTIANS AND PASTORS FROM DELU-
SIONS AND DECEPTIONS ABOUT WHO THEY ARE.

It shows us what we are to do to please the Lord.

But be ye doers of the word, and not hearers only, deceiving your own selves.

James 1:22

The prophet Isaiah thought he was good enough. His messages in the first five chapters of Isaiah were very strong against the people. He would often say, "Woe unto them."

Woe unto them that rise up early in the morning, that they may follow strong drink; that continue until night, till wine inflame them!

Isaiah 5:11

Woe unto them that draw iniquity with cords of vanity, and sin as it were with a cart rope:

Isaiah 5:18

Woe unto them that call evil good, and good evil; that put darkness for light, and light for darkness; that put bitter for sweet, and sweet for bitter!

Isaiah 5:20

Woe unto them that are wise in their own eyes, and prudent in their own sight!

Isaiah 5:21

Woe unto them that are mighty to drink wine, and men of strength to mingle strong drink:

Isaiah 5:22

One day, God decided to reveal Himself to Isaiah. Isaiah was shocked when his real condition was revealed by God. All it took was one glimpse of God in His glory. Immediately, Isaiah was delivered from his delusions. He changed his message at once. He said, "Woe is unto me!" He no longer said, "Woe is unto them."

Then said I, Woe is me! for I am undone; because I am a man of unclean lips, and I dwell in the midst of a people of unclean lips: for mine eyes have seen the King, the Lord of hosts.

Isaiah 6:5

As we correct people and see other people's faults all the time, may God help us to see our own failings. May we see ourselves the way God sees us. Do not be impressed by what people say to you. Do not receive the flattery of human beings. What is highly esteemed in the sight of men is often an abomination in the sight of God.

And he said unto them, Ye are they which justify yourselves before men; but God knoweth your hearts: for that which is highly esteemed among men is abomination in the sight of God.

Luke 16:15

Once I thought I was doing well in the ministry. The Lord revealed Himself to me in a vision and showed me a picture of some greasy faeces. Then He told me that, that was what I looked like to Him. I was full of sorrow for my pathetic condition and I wept before the Lord. I wondered why the Lord had anything to do with me. You see, most people, including myself, thought I was doing well. Dear friend, a regular time with God will save you from delusions.

The Word of God is like that. God shows Himself to you. Every time you read the Word of God, you see God. When Isaiah saw the Lord, he had no deceptions about what he was. Pray that God will reveal Himself to you as you read the Bible everyday. Many church members would not be as proud, arrogant and presumptuous as they are if they knew what they looked like before God. Many Christians would not accuse their leaders if they had just a glimpse at what they were really like in the sight of God.

The Word of God is a mirror. It will show us the real picture. A quiet time will reveal the truth to you every time.

We are so subject to delusions and deceptions that we need a regular input of the Word of God in our lives. I cannot overemphasize the need for regularity for the ministration of the Word in our lives. Only a quiet time can give you the regular input that is needed for a constant deliverance from deception.

8. A DAILY QUIET TIME WILL GIVE GREAT SPIRITUAL GROWTH.

A daily quiet time exposes you regularly to spiritual food. The Word of God is milk for your soul (1 Peter 2:2). It is bread for the hungry (Matthew 4:4) and it is meat for the men (Hebrews 5:12) and it is sweeter than honey for dessert (Psalm 19:10).

Charismatic churches are full of thousands of undeveloped spiritual babies. The pastors of today's charismatic churches are seen by their members as superstars who have the answers to everything. This is not the case. Perhaps we pastors enjoy having people depend on us. They look to us as though we are semi-gods with a panacea for every problem.

When I was growing up as a Christian, I belonged to a Scripture Union fellowship. I did not belong to a large charismatic church. There was no superstar TV personality pastor in SU fellowship. We were directed to the Word of God as the source of everything. I am so grateful that the first thing I learnt in the Scripture Union was to have a daily quiet time. I remember the day I was taught to have a daily quiet time. Little did I know that I was being directed towards the most important thing in Christianity - the Word of God. I was being shown how to receive milk on a daily basis, meat and bread for all my needs and something sweeter than honey when I wanted something sweet.

A spiritual x-ray of a large charismatic church will reveal tiny undeveloped Christians who shout Christian slogans and clichés and hail their pastors as though they were pop stars or soccer heroes. Is it any wonder that Christianity today is a far cry from what it used to be? There is very little sacrifice. There is very little advancement of the kingdom. And there is so much carnality. Carnality is a sign of immaturity. Why is so much of the Body of Christ immature? Because most Christians do not have a daily quiet time.

Christians today depend on a quick microwave snack from their pastors' Bibles on Sunday morning. Is there any comparison between a child who has a balanced meal every day and someone who has a quick microwave thirty-five minute sermon snack every other week? It's time to grow. It's time to benefit from the milk, bread, meat and honey that is in your Bible. Having a daily quiet time is the best habit I learned as a Christian.

9. A DAILY QUIET TIME BRINGS INNER HEALING.

He sent his word, and healed them, and delivered them from their destructions.

Psalm 107:20

The Word of God has a way of healing us of our pain and wounds. God will touch you where it hurts if you will allow Him. And He will heal you of every situation in your life.

Spiritual, emotional and psychological problems are the most difficult to solve. Doctors often struggle with these problems to no avail. The diagnosis and treatment of spiritual, emotional and psychological problems are one of the most difficult areas for medicine. But God has a solution. The solution is in His Word. A daily dose of God's powerful Word will bring healing to every inner wound. What did Jesus say? 'The Spirit of the Lord is upon me because He has anointed me to preach the gospel to the poor; he hath sent me to heal the broken hearted… (Luke. 4:18). How was Jesus going to heal the broken hearted? Through the Word of God!

10. A DAILY QUIET TIME BRINGS HEALING TO THE BODY.

My son, attend to my words; incline thine ear unto my sayings. Let them not depart from thine eyes; keep them in the midst of thine heart. For they are life unto those that find them, and health [medicine] to all their flesh.

Proverbs 4:20-22

The Hebrew word for health is, 'marpe', which means, 'medicine.'

It may sound difficult to believe but God's Word actually brings healing to our physical bodies. The Bible says that they are life and health to the flesh. The flesh means the physical body.

I will like to quote to you a very interesting article I read in Reader's Digest:

[30] *The notion that religious faith can promote physical well-being is not new. Most of us have heard of cases in which someone, seemingly by sheer faith and will, has miraculously recovered from a terminal illness or survived far longer than*

doctors thought possible. What is new is that such rewards of religion are becoming the stuff of science.

"We cannot prove scientifically that God heals, but I believe we can prove that belief in God has a beneficial effect," declares Dale A. Matthew, M.D., Associate Professor of Medicine at Georgetown University "There's little doubt that healthy religious faith and practices can help people get better."

Compelling Evidence

Just how powerful is the evidence linking faith and health? More than 30 studies have found a connection between spiritual or religious commitment and longer life. Among the most compelling: A survey of 5,286 Californians found that church members have lower death rates than non-members, regardless of risk factors such as smoking, drinking, obesity, and inactivity.

Those with a religious commitment had fewer symptoms or had better health outcomes in seven out of eight cancer studies, four out of five blood pressure studies, four out of six heart disease studies, and four out of five general health studies.

People with a strong religious commitment seem to be less prone to depression, suicide, alcoholism, and other addictions, according to one research analysis.

One of the most extensive reviews demonstrates that the connections between religion and health cut across age, sex, cultural, and geographic boundaries. It includes more than 200 studies in which religion was found to be a factor in the incidence of a disease, explains Jeffrey S. Levin, a former professor at Eastern Virginia Medical School in Norfolk. Levin found an association between good health and religion in studies of children and older adults; of U.S. Protestants, European Catholics, Japanese Buddhists, and Israeli Jews; of people living in the 1930's and 1980's; of patients suffering from acute and chronic diseases.

How Prayer Heals

Why does faith appear to have such a powerful protective effect? Experts offer several possible explanations.

Going to religious services guarantees contact with people. Social support is a well-documented key to health and longevity.

Faith gives a sense of hope and control that counteracts stress. "Commitment to a system of beliefs enables people to better handle traumatic illness, suffering, and loss," says Harold G. Koenig, M.D., director of the center for the study of religion, spirituality, and health at Duke University Medical Center.

Praying evokes beneficial changes in the body. When people pray, they experience the same decreases in blood pressure, metabolism, heart and breathing rates as the famous "relaxation response" described by Herbert Benson, M.D. of the Harvard Medical School. Reciting the rosary, for example, involves the same steps as the relaxation response: repeating a word, prayer, phrase, or sound, and returning to the repetition when other thoughts intrude. While the relaxation response works regardless of the words used, Benson says, those who choose a religious phrase are more likely to benefit if they believe in God.

Can Others' Prayers Heal?

Researchers are investigating whether the prayers of others can heal. Benson and his colleagues, studying coronary-bypass patients, and Matthews, studying people with rheumatoid arthritis, are trying to confirm findings of an oft-quoted 1988 study by cardiologist Randolph Byrd, M.D.

Dr. Byrd divided 393 heart patients in San Francisco General Hospital Medical Center into two groups. One was prayed for by Christians around the country; the other did not receive prayers from study participants. Patients did not know to which group they belonged. The group that was prayed for experienced fewer complications, fewer cases of pneumonia, fewer cardiac arrests, less congestive heart failure, and needed fewer antibiotics.

Even more confounding are controversial studies suggesting prayer can influence everything from the growth of bacteria in a lab to healing wounds in mice. "These studies on lower organisms can be done with great scientific precision, and the findings can't be explained away by, say, the placebo effect," says Larry Dossey, M.D., author of Prayer Is Good Medicine.

Doctors as Believers

Dr. Dossey became so convinced of the power of prayer that he began to pray privately for his patients. Nevertheless, he and other experts tread cautiously in this area. "We certainly don't want to start selling religion in the name of science," he says. "People need to make their own choices."

And yet, health care institutions are beginning to pay attention to the faith-health connection. Conferences on spirituality and health have been sponsored by Harvard Medical School and the Mayo Clinic. Nearly half of U.S. medical schools now offer courses on the topic. In a survey of 269 doctors at the 1996 meeting of the American Academy of Family Physicians, 99% said they thought religious beliefs could contribute to healing. When asked about their personal experiences, 63% of doctors said God intervened to improve their own medical conditions.

Clearly, their patients agree that prayer is a powerful tool in healing. Polls by Time/CNN and USA Weekend show that about 80% of Americans believe spiritual faith or prayer can help people recover from illness or injury, and more than 60% think doctors should talk to patients about faith and even pray with those who request it.

This yearning for a connection between religion and medicine is partly a reaction to a health care system that has become increasingly rushed and impersonal. "In medicine, the pendulum had swung so far toward the physical that it almost totally excluded anything spiritual," Dr. Dossey says. "This didn't feel right to patients or many physicians, and the pendulum has begun to swing back."

How Faith Fits In

So what does this mean for the average person? It does not mean adding worship to the list of healthy things you can do. You can't adopt faith as you would a low-fat diet.

What you can do is speak up if you're facing illness or surgery and would like your belief to be part of your health care. That doesn't mean you should expect your doctor to pray with or for you. But it's reasonable to expect him to listen to your needs, arrange a visit from the hospital chaplain, or allow time for prayer before you're wheeled into the operating room.

"Faith" Koenig maintains, "offers people some control over their lives as opposed to just depending on a medical profession that's becoming more distant and mechanized every day."[30]

11. A DAILY QUIET TIME CAUSES CLEANSING.

Now ye are clean through the word which I have spoken unto you.

John 15:3

Sanctify them through thy truth: thy word is truth.

John 17:17

As Isaiah said, "We have unclean lips and we dwell in the midst of unclean people." Thank God that a daily quiet time provides cleansing. Have you ever wondered why there is very little of God's power in the Church today? It is because of the sin and the filth that is in the Church.

For this ye know, that no whoremonger, nor unclean person, nor covetous man, who is an idolater, hath any inheritance in the kingdom of Christ and of God. Let no man deceive you with vain words: for because of these things cometh the wrath of God upon the children of disobedience.

Ephesians 5:5,6

12. A DAILY QUIET TIME PRODUCES FAITH IN THE AVERAGE CHRISTIAN.

So then faith cometh by hearing, and hearing by the word of God.

Romans 10:17

Faith comes by hearing and hearing by the Word of God. The more you read the Bible, the more you will believe in God's power to save. The Bible is littered with hundreds of stories of God's deliverance. You will see people at the brink of death who were saved by God. You will read about people in difficult and complex situations who were saved by the power of God. These testimonies inspire faith. Do not take it for granted. Do not think that you know everything about God. A daily dose of the Word of God will increase your faith.

13. A DAILY QUIET TIME DRIVES AWAY
WEARINESS, DEJECTION AND DEPRESSION.

For as the rain cometh down, and the snow from heaven, and returneth not thither, but watereth the earth, and maketh it bring forth and bud, that it may give seed to the sower, and bread to the eater:

Isaiah 55:10

The Word of God is like rain and snow that cools and refreshes. You will be blessed by the cooling and refreshing effect of a daily quiet time. As I go about I often become weary and unhappy if I have not been able to have time with the Lord. I cannot explain it. You have to experience it for yourself. The refreshing and calming effect that a time in the presence of God produces cannot be compared with anything.

14. A DAILY QUIET TIME PRODUCES POWER
FOR THE ORDINARY CHRISTIAN.

For I am not ashamed of the gospel of Christ: for it is the power of God unto salvation to every one that believeth; to the Jew first, and also to the Greek.

Romans 1:16

The gospel of Jesus Christ (which is the Word of God) is the power of God unto salvation. There is power in the Word of God. There is healing in the Word of God. When you expose yourself to the Word of God you are exposing yourself to a supernatural power. God is actually in His Word. He is the Word. "In the beginning was the Word and the Word was with God and the Word was God." God is the Word or the Word is God. Expose yourself to the Word and you are exposing yourself to God. The power of God will be real to you.

What power is able to change the lives of thousands of young people who would have been dancing, drinking, smoking and infecting each other with HIV? I am not talking about elderly men and women without any life or strength. I am talking about young men and women who are changed by the power of God's Word.

Someone once said of my church, "Your church is like a large youth group." You see, my church is made up of mostly young people. I have thousands of young people who serve the Lord with all their heart, might and strength. What has changed the course of their lives? Is it the laying on of hands? Is it fasting? No! It is the Word of God. The Word of God is the power of God with the ability to save and to change.

15. A DAILY QUIET TIME CAN MAKE YOU WISER THAN YOUR ENEMIES, YOUR TEACHERS AND THE ELDERS.

Thou through thy commandments hast made me wiser than mine enemies: for they are ever with me. I have more understanding than all my teachers: for thy testimonies are my meditation. I understand more than the ancients, because I keep thy precepts.

Psalm 119:98-100

105

A daily quiet time will give you the right perspective of life. You will be delivered from delusions about what life has to offer. It will guide you and convert your soul. You will see life from a different perspective. A daily quiet time will make you wiser than the average person around you.

Recently, I was walking on some huge golf courses that belonged to a single Japanese man. As I looked at the vast amount of land that belonged to this gentleman, I hoped that this man knew God. You see, one day he will have to leave this earth and leave the vast properties that he owns.

The Word of God makes you value what is truly valuable. The Word of God makes you see the wealth of this world in the right perspective. Jesus said, "Lay up for yourself treasures in heaven." (Matthew 6:20). When the Word of God is in you, you will say to yourself, "I will lay up for myself treasures in heaven," - that is true wisdom.

CHAPTER TWELVE

Don't Lose Your Only Chance For A Personal Relationship With God

Not every one that saith unto me, Lord, Lord, shall enter into the kingdom of heaven; but he that doeth the will of my Father which is in heaven. Many will say to me in that day, Lord, Lord, have we not prophesied in thy name? and in thy name have cast out devils? and in thy name done many wonderful works? And then will I profess unto them, I never knew you: depart from me, ye that work iniquity.

Matthew 7:21-23

One of the least understood statements of Jesus is, "I never knew you." These people were prophesying in His name. They were doing many wonderful works in His name but Jesus said, "I never knew you." I have always wondered how it is possible to do the work of God without knowing God. Dear friend, you had better believe what Jesus said.

It is possible to be a member of a church and to do great things for God but not know God. A daily quiet time will make you have a personal relationship with the Lord. Nothing else can make you have a personal relationship with the Lord. Coming to church a thousand times is different from having a personal one to one interaction with the Lord. It is this personal interaction with the Lord which most Christians lack.

It seems that God is more interested in the personal relationship than the great public works that we do in His name. A quiet time will make you have that personal knowledge of God. A daily quiet time will prevent you from going to hell. A quiet time will save you from the delusion that working for God is the same as knowing Him. There are people who work for me but don't know me personally. I have employees who hardly know me. They may recognize me when I come around, but they do not have a personal relationship with me.

I have many shepherds and pastors who work in the church with me. But I do not have a personal relationship with all of them. Definitely, there is a difference between those who just work for me and those who have a personal relationship with me.

How come I have a personal relationship with some of my pastors and shepherds? The answer is simple.

Some of these pastors and shepherds make the effort to be close to me and to interact with me personally. Now I know them personally and can even call them friends. There are people in my church who do wonderful works in the name of the church or on my behalf. But the reality is that I don't know them personally.

Earlier on, when someone would ask me how they could do better in the ministry, I would give them twenty-five principles for church growth and then I would show them eighteen strategies for effective evangelism. I might show them seven steps to an excellent ministry. But now, if you ask me that same question I would say, "Just draw closer to God and know Him personally." You see, there is no point in running around on His behalf when you do not know Him personally.

It is time to know Him personally. It is said that pastors worldwide pray an average of seven minutes a day. If the pastors are spending less than ten minutes with their Heavenly Father, then perhaps the ordinary members are spending a few seconds every week with their Lord. It is no wonder the Church is the way it is.

It is time to know Him personally. The only way is to have a regular daily quiet time. Do you expect God to come to you to develop a relationship with you? Certainly not! It is up to you and I to draw near to Him on a daily basis.

Draw nigh to God, and he will draw nigh to you...

James 4:8

In this regard, a daily quiet time may actually be your passport to heaven.

When you meet someone in public and shake his hand you can hardly say you know him. In my home, I have a picture which my mother-in-law took with President Clinton, former president of the USA. When she showed it to us, we said, "Wow, when did you meet him? How did you get to know him?"

She smiled and told us about how she had a brief interaction with him and managed to take a picture with him at a conference. The picture gives an impression that he knows her. But the reality is that he doesn't know her at all, and she doesn't know him either. Meeting someone in public does not mean that you know him at all.

Knowing about someone is different from knowing the person. There are many people who know about me but do not know me. Some people who see me from afar may have the impression that I am proud. Some people may hear me speak and think that I am a difficult person. May God forgive me for my sins. However, some people who know me personally may have a different impression.

Knowing God from afar is very different from knowing Him personally. Your impressions from afar will only change when you get closer to Him. The way you can develop that personal relationship with God is not in public at the church service. You do not develop a personal relationship with God by attending conventions and crusades. You cannot develop a personal relationship with anyone by interacting in public. There has to be communication at a personal level. There has to be a personal interaction! There has to be a quiet time. You can know God personally by spending time with Him during your quiet time.

CHAPTER THIRTEEN

Avoid Shallowness By the Power of Quiet Time

And these are they likewise which are sown on stony ground; who, when they have heard the word, immediately receive it with gladness; And have no root in themselves, and so endure but for a time: afterward, when affliction or persecution ariseth for the word's sake, immediately they are offended.

Mark 4:16,17

Shallowness is the disease of the charismatic Christian. A lot of talk but no depth. Even our churches are shallow and without depth. A shallow end without depth. I once visited a place near the Sahara Desert. I was amazed that there were only a few charismatic or pentecostal churches there. You see, for all our noise, we the charismatic and Pentecostal churches have no real outreach to the places of greatest need. So it is with the Christians. We are loud, noisy, "praisey" people with lots of positive confessions. And yet, there is little depth in most of us. It is time to come out of shallowness.

SEVEN SYMPTOMS OF SHALLOWNESS IN CHRISTIANS

1. A LACK OF KNOWLEDGE OF THE SCRIPTURES.

Many charismatic Christians do not know what the Bible says. We conducted an exam in one of our churches. Here came a gentleman who claimed to be a shepherd/leader. I gave him a Bible and said to him, "Show me where the Bible speaks about the resurrection." This gentleman could not find where the Bible talked about the resurrection. This is truly a symptom of shallowness. People are in churches shouting and singing but they have no depth. No wonder charismatic Christians are easily swayed by the next wave of sensationalism.

2. INABILITY TO QUOTE SCRIPTURE.

Quoting scriptures is different from knowing where things are in the Bible. Any Christian of depth will be able to quote Scriptures. Every Christian should have a version of the Bible from which he quotes accurately.

I was recently preaching in a very large charismatic church and I began to ask questions. I said to one, "Please quote John 1:12." I said to another, "Please quote 2 Corinthians 5:17." I said to yet another, "What is Romans 6:23?"

Amazingly, most of the Christians who fill charismatic churches cannot quote these Scriptures. Yet, these are some of the basic scriptures for every believer's foundation. There can be no progress with God unless we have depth. Scripture memorization is essential. Jesus Christ memorized scripture.

In Matthew 4 when the devil tempted Jesus, He accurately quoted Scriptures from Deuteronomy and paralysed the devil with them.

3. INABILITY TO PRAY FOR AT LEAST ONE HOUR A DAY.

Shallowness is caused by failure to interact with the Lord. Anyone who has some depth with God spends at least an hour every day in the presence of the Lord. When you know God one hour will be too short for you. Conduct a survey in any large charismatic church. Ask how many Christians have spent at least one hour in prayer and Bible reading on that day. You will find out that very few people spend more than a few seconds with God. No wonder most of them are shallow and don't know God.

4. INABILITY TO LEAD AND TEACH AFTER BEING A CHRISTIAN FOR TWO YEARS.

For when for the time ye ought to be teachers, ye have need that one teach you again which be the first principles of the oracles of God; and are become such as have need of milk, and not of strong meat.

Hebrews 5:12

After someone has been a believer for some time he is expected to also share the things he has received. Paul clearly said that

113

there is a time when a believer is expected to be a teacher. *"For when for the time ye ought to be teachers, ye have need that one teach you again..."* (Hebrews 5:12).

The failure of the majority of believers to rise into Christian leadership is simply a sign of shallowness in the congregation.

5. A LACK OF INTEREST IN CHRISTIAN BOOKS AND TAPES.

Shallow Christians rarely read Christian books. A Christian book will take you deeper than you are. It will take you higher in the Lord. Show me someone who reads Christian books and listens to tapes and I will show you someone who is going deeper with the Lord.

6. INABILITY TO WORSHIP GOD.

I will give you an assignment. Next time you go to church, look around and see how many are singing the songs. Many of the Christians do not even know the songs. They mumble and stumble along as the worship leader leads the congregation. The reality is that they do not know God and have no personal desire to worship Him. It's just a part of the service that has to run its course. They wait for the entertainment that will come from the pastor's jokes. Ask yourself, "Am I a worshipper?" Can you sing the song alone in your home?

7. INABILITY TO FELLOWSHIP REGULARLY.

The shallowness of many Christians is once again manifested in their inability to regularly fellowship with the Lord and with others.

But if we walk in the light, as he is in the light, we have fellowship one with another, and the blood of Jesus Christ his Son cleanseth us from all sin.

1 John 1:7

They struggle to attend church every Sunday and often arrive late. It is almost as though they have a chore to do. Let me ask you a question. When a man is developing a personal relationship with a woman does he not enjoy interacting with her? Does he not long to see her again? The deeper the relationship the greater the interaction will be.

We will have a deep relationship with our God as we have a daily quiet time. Shallowness will be taken away from the church and Christianity will have more meaning for us all.

CHAPTER FOURTEEN

Obtain Wisdom Keys Through The Power Of Quiet Time

1. A QUIET TIME WILL SHOW YOU THAT THERE ARE TWO KINDS OF WISDOM: HUMAN CLEVERNESS AND THE WISDOM OF GOD.

Who is a wise man and endued with knowledge among you? let him show out of a good conversation his works with meekness of wisdom. But if ye have bitter envying and strife in your hearts, glory not, and lie not against the truth. This wisdom descendeth not from above, but is earthly, sensual, devilish. For where envying and strife is, there is confusion and every evil work. But the wisdom that is from above is first pure, then peaceable, gentle, and easy to be entreated, full of

mercy and good fruits, without partiality, and
without hypocrisy.

James 3:13-17

2. A QUIET TIME WILL SHOW YOU THAT HUMAN CLEVERNESS
IS A POOR SUBSTITUTE FOR THE WISDOM OF GOD.

Where is the wise? where is the scribe? where is
the disputer of this world? hath not God made
foolish the wisdom of this world? For after that in
the wisdom of God the world by wisdom knew not
God, it pleased God by the foolishness of preaching to save them that believe. For the Jews
require a sign, and the Greeks seek after wisdom:
But we preach Christ crucified, unto the Jews a
stumblingblock, and unto the Greeks foolishness; But unto them which are called, both Jews
and Greeks, Christ the power of God, and the wisdom of God. Because the foolishness of God is
wiser than men; and the weakness of God is
stronger than men.

1 Corinthians 1:20-25

3. A QUIET TIME MAKES YOU MOVE PROGRESSIVELY AWAY FROM
HUMAN CLEVERNESS AND TOWARDS THE WISDOM OF GOD.

Let no man deceive himself. If any man among
you seemeth to be wise in this world, let him
become a fool, that he may be wise. For the wisdom of this world is foolishness with God. For it

is written, He taketh the wise in their own crafti-
ness.

1 Corinthians 3:18,19

And it came to pass in those days, that he went out
into a mountain to pray, and continued all night in
prayer to God. And when it was day, he called unto
him his disciples: and of them he chose twelve,
whom also he named apostles; Simon, (whom he
also named Peter,) and Andrew his brother, James
and John, Philip and Bartholomew, Matthew and
Thomas, James the son of Alphaeus, and Simon
called Zelotes, And Judas the brother of James,
and Judas Iscariot, which also was the traitor.

Luke 6:12-16

4. A QUIET TIME INTRODUCES YOU TO REAL WISDOM
BECAUSE YOU BEGIN TO FEAR, RESPECT AND OBEY GOD.

The fear of the Lord is the beginning of wisdom:
and the knowledge of the holy is understanding.

Proverbs 9:10

The fear of the Lord is the beginning of wisdom: a
good understanding have all they that do his
commandments: his praise endureth for ever.

Psalm 111:10

And unto man he said, Behold, the fear of the
Lord, that is wisdom; and to depart from evil is
understanding.

Job 28:28

**5. THE QUIET TIME IS THE KEY TO GOD'S WISDOM
AND THEREFORE TO YOUR PROMOTION.**

Wisdom is the principal thing; therefore get wisdom: and with all thy getting get understanding.

Proverbs 4:7

**6. BY HAVING A QUIET TIME YOU EXALT WISDOM IN YOUR LIFE
AND THEREFORE BRING YOURSELF TO HONOUR.**

Exalt her, and she shall promote thee: she shall bring thee to honour, when thou dost embrace her.

Proverbs 4:8

**7. A QUIET TIME IS YOUR KEY TO WISDOM
AND THEREFORE YOUR KEY TO VICTORY.**

Wisdom is better than weapons of war: but one sinner destroyeth much good.

Ecclesiastes 9:18

And they were not able to resist the wisdom and the spirit by which he spake.

Acts 6:10

Then shall the lame man leap as an hart, and the tongue of the dumb sing: for in the wilderness shall waters break out, and streams in the desert.

Isaiah 35:6

This book of the law shall not depart out of thy mouth; but thou shalt meditate therein day and night, that thou mayest observe to do according

to all that is written therein: for then thou shalt make thy way prosperous, and then thou shalt have good success.

Joshua 1:8

8. A QUIET TIME IS YOUR KEY TO BECOMING WEALTHY BECAUSE YOU HAVE ACCESS TO THE WISDOM OF GOD.

Riches and honour are with me; yea, durable riches and righteousness. That I may cause those that love me to inherit substance; and I will fill their treasures.

Proverbs 8:18,21

Length of days is in her right hand; and in her left hand riches and honour.

Proverbs 3:16

The crown of the wise is their riches...

Proverbs 14:24

CHAPTER FIFTEEN

Insist On A Daily Prayer Time

Quiet time is not only a time of Bible reading and study but also a time of daily prayer. No matter how important you are, you need to communicate daily with the Lord. There are some Christians who only pray but do not study the Word. Such people cannot develop a wholesome relationship with God. It is a combination of the Word and prayer that builds up a daily prayer time.

ELEVEN REASONS FOR DAILY PRAYER

1. PRAYER IS VERY IMPORTANT.

Someone once said that it is more important to know how to pray than to have a degree from the university.

There are many things that are important in this life. A good education is important. Money is important. A good marriage is important. But, a good prayer life is most important!

Let this enter your spirit - In all your getting, get prayer! In all your activities, make room for prayer!

2. GREAT MEN LIKE DANIEL PRAYED DURING THEIR QUIET TIME.

Now when Daniel knew that the writing was signed, he went into his house; and his windows being open in his chamber toward Jerusalem, he kneeled upon his knees three times a day, and prayed, and gave thanks before his God, as he did aforetime.

Daniel 6:10

You will notice from this scripture that Daniel prayed three times a day. An important phrase used in this verse is "as he did aforetime". That means that Daniel had been praying these prayers on a regular basis. Daniel was not just praying because he was in trouble; he had a habit of prayer.

Many times when people become prosperous they stop going for prayer meetings and eventually backslide. Not so with Daniel! He was the Prime Minister of his country, second in authority only to the king. He was a successful man who had risen from slavery to the high office of Prime Minister. He was one of the most respected and feared men in the nation. He was a major politician of the day. He was a civil servant. Yet, he prayed three times a day, everyday!

3. No one is ever too busy, too blessed or too successful to pray.

You may have a busy lifestyle and you may be a very important person, however; I do not think that you are busier than Daniel was. Daniel was a Prime Minister, a leader in the nation. Many people think that Heads of State and Ministers of government have a relaxed and enjoyable life, flying all over the world. That is not true!

I am the head of a large organization myself, and I know that people in high positions do not have an easy life. **The higher you go, the greater the responsibility you have.**

There is so much hard work involved in staying on the cutting edge of life and ministry. Did you know that successful executives like Daniel are so stressed out that they are prone to diseases like stomach ulcers and heart attacks? These conditions are more common with very busy people because of the hard work that they do.

Daniel was one such person. He was a Prime Minister, yet he felt that he was not too busy to pray three times a day. **If you think you are too busy to pray, then you are deceiving yourself.** If you do not pray, it is because you do not want to pray. It is because you do not think that prayer is important now! Daniel was successful, yet he prayed. Why was he able to pray three times a day?

I have watched people in the church rise out of poverty into mega blessings. When they were poor, they had a lot of time to attend prayer meetings. But when they became blessed, they felt everything was all right. No! Everything is not all right! Your state of blessing is not the signal to stop praying!

4. DAILY PRAYER IS OUR SOURCE OF POWER AND PROTECTION.

You must realize that it is prayer that releases the power of God on our behalf. Jesus knew the power of prayer. That is why He spent long hours in prayer.

Maybe you are a successful businessman, and you do not think that you need any of this spiritual "stuff". Perhaps you are a politician and you think your protection must come from fetish or occult powers. Let me tell you right now, there is power in prayer. We do not need any other power when we have the power of prayer. There is protection for us when we pray. The last part of the armor of God is prayer (Ephesians 6: 18). In other words, prayer is an important part of your spiritual defense.

In Ghana, many people become afraid when they prosper. They feel that somebody may use supernatural powers to try to kill them. You have nothing to fear when you are a prayerful person like Daniel. Many people wanted to kill Daniel. These people did not just think about killing Daniel, they actually plotted to eliminate him. Through the power of prayer, Daniel was protected from the lions. I see all the lions in your life scattering away in fear! I see your prayer power rising! I see you going forward because of a newfound prayer life!

...that Jesus also being baptized, and praying, the heaven was opened,

Luke 3:21

I see the heavens opening over your life! Never forget this! The heavens opened when Jesus prayed. Both physical and spiritual blessings rain upon you when you are a prayerful person.

5. DAILY PRAYER IS IMPORTANT TO ACQUIRE AND SUSTAIN THE BLESSINGS OF GOD.

Do you have anything that you are proud of? Have you achieved anything in this life? Let me tell you that it is by the grace of God. By the power of prayer, you will achieve many great things. It is by prayer that you will sustain what God has placed in your hands.

I know of people who were given thousands of dollars as gifts. Today, that money has disappeared into thin air. God may give you something but it also takes His grace to sustain that blessing. Are you the pastor of a great ministry? Let me tell you, it takes prayer to sustain you in the ministry. Why do you think Jesus kept running away to pray?

There is a law of degeneration at work in the world. Everything is decaying. Your business is decaying. Your church is decaying. Your very life is decaying. It takes the power of God, through prayer, to preserve everything that God has given to you.

6. DAILY QUIET TIME PRAYER IS THE MOST EFFECTIVE BECAUSE IT IS HABITUAL.

A man called Dostoyevsky said, **"The second half of a man's life is made up of the habits he acquired in the first half."**

Pascal said, **"The strength of a man's virtues is made up of his habitual acts."**

If you are going to be a great person in this life, you need to have good habits. An action becomes a habit when it is repeated many times; sometimes consciously, sometimes unconsciously. It becomes your custom!

Habits can be either good or bad. Remember that good habits are repeated as easily as bad habits.

A good habit will lead to consistent breakthroughs even without intending to. Bad habits will also lead to consistent failure. If you decide to develop a habit of prayer, you are developing a habit for success.

Jesus went to church on the Sabbath because it was His habit. The Bible tells us that Jesus had customs or habits.

> **...as his custom [habit] was, he went into the synagogue on the sabbath day...**
>
> Luke 4:16

Daniel had a custom of praying three times a day.

> **...he [Daniel] kneeled upon his knees three times a day, and prayed...**
>
> Daniel 6:10

Life in the secular world is not designed to include a prayer time. Work starts early in the morning and continues late into the night. Weeks may pass before you even think of prayer. For many people, it is only an impossible situation that reminds them of the need for prayer. Dear friend, it is important for you to include prayer in your life.

God is not a spare tyre! A spare tyre is something that is never used except in emergencies. God is no fool. Whatsoever a man sows, he will reap. If you have time for God on a regular basis, He will have time to bless you on a regular basis. Only the mercy of God makes Him listen to some of our prayers.

Develop your prayer life until it happens spontaneously. Develop your prayer life until you pray habitually without even thinking of what you are doing.

I MADE TIME TO PRAY

When I was a medical student, I was very busy with my course-work. There was no time to pray at all. But because I had made prayer a part of my Christian life, there was no way I could do without it! I had to somehow include it in my schedule. I decided to pray late at night. I was usually so sleepy that I had to walk about just to stay awake. Prayer was so important to me that I could not leave it out of my life.

One night, as I headed for my room after one of such prayer times, I actually fell asleep whilst walking! It was only when I bumped into the wall of the Spanish Department building of the university that I woke up from my sleep! I believe that God saw my earnest desire to keep praying in spite of an impossible medical school schedule.

7. QUIET TIME PRAYER WILL SUSTAIN YOU IN TROUBLED TIMES.

Why do we wait for trouble before we pray? Would you take someone as a serious friend if he only called you when he was in serious trouble? In times of peace, he had no time for you.

God is looking for someone who will fellowship with Him in both good and bad times.

The more I preach, the better I become at preaching. The more you pray, the better you will become at prayer. In times of crises, you will find yourself rising up to the occasion and delivering powerful prayers that bring results.

8. QUIET TIME PRAYER IS NEEDED FOR NATIONAL LEADERS.

There is no doubt that the world is ruled by wicked spirits in high places. The earth is covered with human beings at war with each other on a daily basis. Famine, wars, epidemics and disasters abound! You just have to keep your eyes on the international news and you will hear about another major disaster.

Dictators of all kinds abound in many nations. Like snakes, which shed their skin, many dictators of yesteryear have a new "democratic look" but are still tyrants and despots at heart. Many national leaders are actually under the influence of evil spirits, and that makes them do the things they do. They cling to power instead of honourably allowing others to have a chance at leadership. Like vampires, they drink the blood of the nation's wealth and stack it away in secret places.

Charismatic leaders like Hitler lead entire nations into initial prosperity, and then eventual destruction through war. I always remember how things changed in South Africa after President De Klerk replaced President Botha. A new leader led to the release of Nelson Mandela and the end of apartheid. It is important for us to pray for these leaders so that our nations prosper. The right person at the helm of affairs will make a lot of difference to our nations. I believe that the presence of a prayerful person like Daniel made a lot of difference to that nation.

9. QUIET TIME PRAYER WILL HELP YOU TO DEVELOP THE ABILITY TO PRAY FOR LONG HOURS.

Years ago, the only prayers I knew about were those that the priests read out to us in church. The longest I could pray was thirty to forty seconds and that was when I recited the Lord's prayer. There were three prayers I knew how to pray: The Lord's Prayer, Hail Mary and a Prayer to the Angel of God! However, as I grew in the Lord I learnt how to pray for myself. I can now pray for several hours at a time.

I always remember the first time I prayed for three hours. I was a student in Achimota School "Prince of Wales College" in Ghana. I was in the midst of a crisis and I needed the intervention of the Lord. I can also remember the first time I prayed for seven hours. I was a sixth former in the same Achimota School. I prayed from 10 a.m. to 5 p.m. I enjoy praying for long hours.

Praying for thirty minutes is almost like no prayer to me. Do not misunderstand me; I am not saying that God does not hear short prayers. I am saying that I have developed the art of praying for long hours like Jesus did. Jesus prayed for three hours in the garden of Gethsemane.

And he went a little farther, and fell on his face, and prayed... And he cometh unto the disciples, and findeth them asleep, and saith unto Peter, WHAT, COULD YE NOT WATCH WITH ME ONE HOUR? He went away again the second time, and

131

prayed... And he came and found them asleep again: for their eyes were heavy. And he left them, and went away again, and prayed the third time, saying the same words.

Matthew 26:39,40,42-44

In this scripture, Jesus was surprised that the disciples could not pray for one hour.

And he cometh unto the disciples, and findeth them asleep, and saith unto Peter, What, could ye not watch with me one hour?

Matthew 26:40

Jesus prayed all night before He chose His disciples.

And it came to pass in those days, that he went out into a mountain to pray, and continued all night in prayer to God. And when it was day, he called unto him his disciples: and of them he chose twelve, whom also he named apostles;

Luke 6:12,13

Long prayer may not be an explicit instruction in the Bible, but it is implicit throughout the Word. In later chapters, I will teach you what to pray about when you decide to pray for long hours.

10. QUIET TIME PRAYER WILL HELP YOU TO DEVELOP A VERY PERSONAL RELATIONSHIP WITH GOD.

Many Christians can only pray when they are in a group. They cannot stay in a room on their own and pray for one hour. That is a great handicap. There is a difference between praying alone and praying with a group of people. Both types of prayer are important.

If you can pray for three hours on your own then you can pray for six hours with other people. It is easier to pray in a group. Each time, you expand your ability to pray alone, you are expanding your ability to chalk great achievements in prayer.

11. QUIET TIME PRAYER WILL HELP YOU TO IMITATE THE PRAYER LIFE OF JESUS.

There are four important times to pray: morning, afternoon, evening and all-the -time.

Jesus prayed in the morning and so do I.

And in the morning, rising up a great while before day, he went out, and departed into a solitary place, and there prayed.

Mark 1:35

What is so important about morning prayer? Prayer in the morning is very good because you meet God before you meet the devil. You meet God before you meet the circumstances of life. God anoints you to overcome every mountain that you will encounter in your life.

Prayer in the afternoon signifies prayer in the midst of activities. When you pray in the afternoon, it signifies that in the heat of the day and in the thick of the battle, you recognize God as the most important force in your life. God will bless you for afternoon prayer. I see you praying in the afternoon!

And when he had sent them away, he departed into a mountain to pray.

Mark 6:46

You can take a little time off your lunch break and pray. That prayer will do you more good than a plate of rice will!

It is also important to pray in the evenings. When the Bible says "watch and pray", it does not mean keep your eyes open when you pray. What it actually means is, stay awake and pray.

And it came to pass in those days, that he went out into a mountain to pray, and continued all night in prayer to God.

Luke 6:12

There is something about praying in the night that is different from praying during the day. It is a very different experience. I have heard stories that witches are very active around 2 a.m. in the night. Perhaps when you pray in the night you are tackling the forces of darkness in a different way. After all, they are called the forces of darkness (night).

The fourth important time to pray is "all-the-time"

Pray without ceasing.

1 Thessalonians 5:17

Prayer is intended to be a never-ending stream of communication with your heavenly Father. He has given us the baptism of the Holy Spirit and the gift of speaking in tongues. I pray all the time. My wife tells me that sometimes I pray in my sleep!

Pray without ceasing.

1 Thessalonians 5:17

You can pray on the bus and on your way to work. You can pray softly undertone when you are in the office. You can pray when you are in the shower. God is happy when His children are constantly in touch with Him.

I have a friend whose wife calls him on his mobile phone at least seven times a day. I have been in meetings with him when he had received not less than four calls from his wife. Nothing important, she was just keeping in touch! I think it is a nice thing. She phones without ceasing!

I see you praying without ceasing! I see you praying in the morning and in the evening! God is changing your life because of your newfound prayer life! Your marriage, business and ministry will never be the same by the time you finish reading this book!

CHAPTER SIXTEEN

Quiet Time is the Most Important Habit of Your Life.

"The second half of a man's life is made up of the habits he acquired in the first half." — *Dostoyevsky*

"The strength of a man's virtues is made up of his habitual acts." — *Pascal*

A habit is something that you do without thinking about it or intending to do it. Every good Christian has many good habits. These good habits are what has made him what he is - a good Christian.

All great men have habits that have made them great. Our Lord Jesus had habits that made Him great.

JESUS CHRIST

1. Going To Church Regularly. Did you know that Jesus had good habits? The Bible teaches us that He had a habit of going to church on the Sabbath day.

> **And he came to Nazareth, where he had been brought up: and, AS HIS CUSTOM WAS, he went into the synagogue on the sabbath day, and stood up for to read.**
>
> Luke 4:16

2. Going On Prayer Retreats. Jesus also had a habit of going to a particular garden for retreats. It was a place that He went often. And everyone knew His habit of praying in the garden.

> **When Jesus had spoken these words, he went forth with his disciples over the brook Cedron, where was a garden, into the which he entered, and his disciples. And Judas also, which betrayed him, knew the place: for JESUS OFTTIMES RESORTED THITHER WITH HIS DISCIPLES.**
>
> John 18:1,2

DANIEL

Daniel prayed at specific times of the day. It was something he was used to doing. It was one of the greatest secrets of his life.

> **Now when Daniel knew that the writing was signed, he went into his house; and his windows being open in his chamber toward Jerusalem, he**

kneeled upon his knees three times a day, and prayed, and gave thanks before his God, AS HE DID AFORETIME.

Daniel 6:10

TEN THINGS EVERY CHRISTIAN SHOULD KNOW ABOUT HABITS

1. A habit is an ACT THAT IS REPEATED EASILY without thinking or planning.

2. A habit is an ACT THAT BECOMES YOUR CUSTOM whether you are conscious of it or not.

3. A habit is often AN INSIGNIFICANT ACT THAT SEEMS TO HAVE NO POWER to affect the future. This is why many people do not recognize the concept of having good habits as a powerful tool for future accomplishments.

4. A habit can EITHER BE GOOD OR BAD, NATURAL OR SPIRITUAL. Spiritual habits are things like morning prayer and having a daily quiet time. Natural habits are things like brushing your teeth and having your daily bath.

5. GOOD HABITS ARE REPEATED AS EASILY AS BAD HABITS.

6. BAD HABITS LEAD TO CONSISTENT FAILURE AND DEFEAT without the person realizing what is happening.

7. GOOD HABITS LEAD TO CONSISTENT SUCCESS AND VICTORY without the person even realizing what he is doing.

8. Bad habits are easy to form but difficult to live with. GOOD HABITS ARE DIFFICULT TO FORM BUT EASY TO LIVE WITH.

9. EVERY SUCCESSFUL CHRISTIAN HAS A NUMBER OF GOOD HABITS THAT have brought him to success. Many years ago, a friend of mine taught me how to have a quiet time with God every morning. I developed that as a personal habit and it has been my greatest secret as a Christian and later as a minister. Almost all the things I preach about come as a result of this good habit.

10. HABITS ARE A SAFETY PROCEDURE FOR CHRISTIANS. This is because even when a leader is under pressure, he will do certain good things habitually, naturally and easily. When under pressure, the leader may not have time to think of what to do or how to act. It is a good habit of prayer or quiet time that may lead him out of difficulty. Just like Jesus, I also have a place I often go to pray. I also often go with my pastors. This habit helps keep me spiritually protected even when I am not aware of danger.

CHAPTER SEVENTEEN

Study The Bible During Your Quiet Time

Study to show thyself approved unto God, a workman that needeth not to be ashamed, rightly dividing the word of truth.

2 Timothy 2:15

These were more noble than those in Thessalonica, in that they received the word with all readiness of mind, and searched the scriptures daily, whether those things were so.

Acts 17:11

For whatsoever things were written aforetime were written for our learning, that we through

patience and comfort of the scriptures might have hope.

Romans 15:4

Oh, the lost art of Bible study! It is sad to see that many Christians do not even read the Bible. Since many people do not read the Bible, they obviously do not study it. In this chapter, I will show you how you can study the Bible effectively.

THREE TYPES OF BIBLE STUDY

1. Microscopic Bible Study - reading very short passages, meditating on single verses and words, and examining the meanings of these verses and words using the English, Greek and Hebrew dictionaries and concordances.

2. Topical Bible Study - this is done by studying individual topics like faith, love, patience and loyalty.

3. Telescopic Bible Study - this involves studying the Bible from a broader perspective.

HOW TO HAVE A MICROSCOPIC BIBLE STUDY

1. Analyse each single word in the verse you are studying.

2. Find out the meaning of every single word in the verse with a dictionary.

3. Check your Bible for any related verses. Analyse these verses also.

4. Look for any corresponding Greek or Hebrew words and find their deep meanings.

5. Ask yourself the following questions:

    i.   What does this verse mean?

    ii. What does this verse mean to me in my specific circumstances?

    iii. What is God telling me personally?

    iv. What is the verse saying?

    v. What is the verse not saying?

    vi. How can I apply it to my life?

    vii. Is there a command for me to obey?

    viii. Is there a warning in the verse for me to heed?

    ix. Is there a good example to follow or a bad example to avoid?

    x. Is there an allegory (story, parable) for me to interpret?

    xi. Is there a promise for me to believe?

    xii. Is there anything for me to pray about?

    xiii. Who can I share this with?

6. Take note of all punctuation and quotation marks.

7. Never take a verse out of context.

HOW TO HAVE A TOPICAL BIBLE STUDY

1. Define the topic using a very good dictionary, e.g. Oxford's or Webster's'. Any topic can be chosen, for example: patience, zeal or love.

2. Look for all the verses that refer to the topic and read them

aloud.

3. Study all these verses microscopically.

4. Find the following:
   i.   The 'Why' and 'Why Not' of the topic.
        For example, "Why have patience?"
        or "Why not have patience?"

   ii. The 'How' and 'How not' of the topic.
        For example, "How do you have patience?"

   iii. The 'Where' and 'Where not' of the topic.
        For example, "Where do you practise love?"
        or "Where don't you practise love?".

   iv. The 'When' and 'When not' of the topic.
        For example, "When should you be zealous?"
        or "When should you not be zealous?"

   v.   The 'What' and 'What not' of the topic.
        For example, "What is love?"
        or "What are the things that are not love?"
        e.g., Love is not sex, sex is not love.

   vi. The 'Who' and 'Who not' of the topic.
        For example, "Who should you be patient with?"
        or "Who should you not be patient with?"

5. Look for types of the topic.
        For example, "What are the types of love?"
        - phileo, agape and eros.

6. Look for examples of the topic.

> Look for examples of patience in the Bible.
> Look for examples of zeal, e.g. Jesus.

7. Look for problems/mistakes related to the topic.

> For example, "what are the problems that come when you don't walk in love? What problems do people have when they don't have patience?"

HOW TO HAVE A TELESCOPIC BIBLE STUDY

1. Read a whole book at a time, preferably in one sitting. Because you are reading large sections it would be easier to read more modern versions of the Bible.

2. Build up a complete picture.

3. Locate the central theme, key verses or passages.

4. Do a microscopic Bible study on key words that you come across.

CHAPTER EIGHTEEN

Tools For An Effective Quiet Time

1. BIBLES

You will need several Bibles to have an effective quiet time. Examples of some good Bibles to have are Dake's Annotated Reference Bible (King James Version), Thompson's Chain Reference Bible (King James Version), New International Version, The Amplified Bible and the New American Standard Bible.

The Bible is God's book for us today. As you read it you will hear the voice of God speaking to you. As you study the Word of God, you will discover new revelations which will affect your life.

2. A NOTEBOOK

And the Lord said unto Moses, Hew thee two tables of stone like unto the first: and I will write

upon these tables the words that were in the first tables, which thou brakest.

Exodus 34:1

You need to write down the things God says to you. I have a book in which I write the things that God shows me. Sometimes I am surprised at the many revelations and instructions that the Lord has given me. I write down the dreams, visions and the words that God gives to me.

3. A Dictionary

Both Oxford's and Webster's dictionaries are good dictionaries to have. You will always be surprised to learn the meanings of words which we often assume we know.

4. A Concordance

Every Christian should have a copy of Strong's Exhaustive Concordance.

5. A Good Attitude

Recognise God as the author.

God, who at sundry times and in divers manners spake in time past unto the fathers by the prophets, Hath in these last days spoken unto us by his Son, whom he hath appointed heir of all things, by whom also he made the worlds;

Hebrews 1:1-2

Focus on Jesus as the central figure in the Bible.

Ought not Christ to have suffered these things, and to enter into his glory? And beginning at Moses and all the prophets, he expounded unto them in all the scriptures the things concerning himself.

Luke 24:26-27

Be willing to receive instructions from the Lord.

All scripture is given by inspiration of God, and is profitable for doctrine, for reproof, for correction, for instruction in righteousness:

2 Timothy 3:16

Allow God to change you.

But we all, with open face beholding as in a glass the glory of the Lord, are changed into the same image from glory to glory, even as by the Spirit of the Lord

2 Corinthians 3:18

CHAPTER NINETEEN

How To Interpret The Bible

It is very important to interpret the Bible correctly when you have your quiet time. The Holy Spirit is the author of the Word of God, therefore He is the one who can lead us into the correct understanding.

> **Knowing this first, that no prophecy of the scripture is of any private interpretation. For the prophecy came not in old time by the will of man: but holy men of God spake as they were moved by the Holy Ghost.**
>
> 2 Peter 1:20,21

NINE KEYS TO INTERPRETING
THE BIBLE CORRECTLY

1. READ THE TEXT IN ITS CONTEXT.

§   Each word must be read in the context of other words in the verse.

§   Each verse must be read in the context of the chapter.

§   Each chapter in the Bible must be read in the context of the whole book.

§   You can make the Bible say almost anything you want it to. Anything that is taken out of its context becomes an oddity. For instance, you can make the Bible say, "There is no God." You may ask, "How do you make the Bible say that there is no God?" Just take four words of Psalm 14:1 out of context of the other words and you will have a false message.

The fool hath said in his heart, There is no God...

Psalm 14:1

When you put the phrase, "There is no God," back in context, you get a different message: "The fool hath said in his heart, there is no God." In other words, it is not a case of "there is no God", but a case of the fool saying in his heart that "there is no God".

If you take some scriptures from the book of Song of Solomon out of context you may even think the Bible is discussing pornography. However, within its context you will discover a beautiful message of the love that God has created.

2. DO NOT SPIRITUALISE MEANINGS OF WORDS.

If you take the language at its face value, you will save yourself from deception. When the Bible says in Matthew 8:17, "By his stripes we are healed," there is no need to spiritualise the meaning of the word 'heal'. The word 'heal' is easily defined in the dictionary. I have reproduced below the meaning of the word "heal" from a dictionary.

heal v. 1 (often followed by up) become sound or healthy again. 2 .cause to heal. 3. put right (differences etc.). 4 alleviate (sorrow etc.). healer n. [Old English: related to whole]

There is no reason to spiritualise or allegorise the meaning of any word. As you can see, the word 'heal' can also mean 'to alleviate sorrow'. In the context of Matthew 8:17 you will notice that Jesus was not trying to alleviate sorrow but He was healing the sicknesses of the multitudes.

> **When the even was come, they brought unto him many that were possessed with devils: and he cast out the spirits with his word, and healed all that were sick: That it might be fulfilled which was spoken by Esaias the prophet, saying, Himself took our infirmities, and bare our sicknesses.**
>
> Matthew 8:16,17

3. BELIEVE WHAT YOU READ.

> **And Moses stretched out his hand over the sea; and the Lord caused the sea to go back by a strong east wind all that night, and made the sea**

dry land, and the waters were divided. And the children of Israel went into the midst of the sea upon the dry ground: and the waters were a wall unto them on their right hand, and on their left.

Exodus 14:21,22

When the Bible says that Moses stretched out his rod over the Red Sea and the sea parted, you must believe that it actually happened. If you spiritualise it you will immediately stray into deceptive waters.

4. FIND OUT THE MEANING OF HEBREW AND GREEK WORDS FROM WHICH THE ENGLISH VERSION WAS TRANSLATED.

Whenever text is being translated from one language to another, there are difficulties in getting the correct words to correspond to fit. We encountered such difficulties when we were translating my books from English to French. I cannot imagine the difficulties the Bible translators encountered when they were translating the Bible from Hebrew and Greek to English.

Interpretation of what God is saying will be clearer when you have the privilege of understanding the language from which the Bible was translated. Going into the Hebrew and Greek is just an attempt to clarify the meaning of what is being transmitted.

5. INTERPRET PUNCTUATION MARKS PROPERLY.

Punctuation marks like full stops, commas, colons and semi-colons have important meanings. When you leave them out you will be subject to error. For instance, a colon means that text ahead explains further what has been said.

6. UNDERSTAND THE BACKGROUND (PERSON, PLACE AND TIME).

It is important to understand the background of the writer. It is even more revelatory to know the time and place of the writing of that letter. For instance, when Paul said to be subject to authorities, he was writing to the Romans. The Romans were being ruled by a very oppressive dictator, the emperor Nero.

Let every soul be subject unto the higher powers. For there is no power but of God: the powers that be are ordained of God. Whosoever therefore resisteth the power, resisteth the ordinance of God: and they that resist shall receive to themselves damnation. For rulers are not a terror to good works, but to the evil. Wilt thou then not be afraid of the power? do that which is good, and thou shalt have praise of the same:

Romans 13.1-3

This instruction is interesting when you understand the circumstances under which believers were operating. God was showing that it was wisdom to be subject to authorities. It is interesting to note that Christianity flourishes more under tyrannical rulers than under democracy. Perhaps this was part of God's wisdom to make people believe in Him.

You should also consider that Paul was writing from prison when he said,

Finally, my brethren, rejoice in the Lord. To write the same things to you, to me indeed is not

grievous, but for you it is safe.

Philippians 3:1

Paul mentions joy fourteen times in the epistle of Philippians. And the key word is 'rejoice'. He taught that Christians were to rejoice in fellowship with one another (Philippians 1:3-11), in afflictions of the gospel (Philippians 1 :12-30), and in ministry for saints (Philippians 2 :1-18). He also taught that Christians should rejoice in faithfulness of ministers (Philippians 2:19-30), in the Lord and not in Judaism (Philippians 3:1-21), unity (Philippians 4:1-4) and always in all things (Philippians 4:4-23).

However, we can misuse this concept of background and get into error. For instance, I was once speaking to a lady. She said to me, "I don't see why I should not commit fornication." I was a bit taken aback. She continued, "I don't see what's wrong with that." "But the Bible says that it is not right," I said. She answered, "But the Bible was written a long time ago. In those days such things were not accepted but society has changed."

This young lady was throwing out the scripture because she wanted to do her own thing. But God's Word is timeless.

Knowing the background, that is, the place, time and writer is not to throw out some scripture as 'inapplicable' but to throw more light on them.

7. CONSIDER SECULAR MATERIAL THAT THROWS MORE LIGHT ON SCRIPTURE.

For instance, historical, archaeological, geographical and cultural materials can give more insight into what the Word of God is saying.

8. Interpret the scripture by scripture.

Interpret each passage in the light of the Bible teaching as a whole. Scripture cannot contradict itself; God cannot contradict Himself. When you see different parts of the Bible which seem to be difficult to understand do not struggle with isolated scriptures. The Bible must be interpreted in the context of other parts of the scriptures.

If you read certain parts of the Old Testament, you may think that God is interested in slaughtering large numbers of people. But if you look at it in the context of other parts of the scripture you will discover that God loves all men and wants all men to be saved.

> **But, beloved, be not ignorant of this one thing, that one day is with the Lord as a thousand years, and a thousand years as one day. The Lord is not slack concerning his promise, as some men count slackness; but is longsuffering to us-ward, not willing that any should perish, but that all should come to repentance.**
>
> 2 Peter 3:8,9

You will also discover that God hates the sin of murder.

> **These six things doth the Lord hate: yea, seven are an abomination unto him: A proud look, a lying tongue, and HANDS THAT SHED INNOCENT BLOOD,**
>
> Proverbs 6:16,17

157

9. ASK THE HOLY SPIRIT TO TEACH YOU HIS WORD.

Ultimately God is the one who can teach you His Word. He has given us the Holy Spirit for that purpose. Ask the Holy Spirit to teach you His Word.

Howbeit when he, the Spirit of truth, is come, he will guide you into all truth: for he shall not speak of himself; but whatsoever he shall hear, that shall he speak: and he will show you things to come.

John 16:13

CHAPTER TWENTY

What Great Men Said About The Bible

31 1. George Washington (1st President of the USA)

"It is impossible to rightly govern the world without God and the Bible."

2. Thomas Jefferson (3rd President of the USA)

"A studious perusal of the sacred volume will make better citizens, better fathers, and better husbands."

3. Andrew Jackson (7th President of the USA)

"That Book, Sir, is the rock on which our republic rests."

4. Woodrow Wilson (28th President of the USA)

"You will know the Bible is the Word of God when you read it: for in it you will find the key to your own heart, your own happiness, and your success. I beg of you that you read it, and find this out for yourselves... A man has deprived himself of the best there is in the world who has deprived himself of this (the knowledge of the Bible)."

159

5. Herbert Hoover (31st President of the USA)

"There is no other book so various as the Bible, nor one so full of concentrated wisdom."

6. Ulysses S. Grant (18th President of the USA)

"To the influence of this book we are indebted to the progress made in civilization, and to this we must look as our guide in the future."

7. Napoleon Bonaparte (Famous French general)

"The Bible is more than a book; it is a living being with an action; a power which invades everything that opposes its extension."

8. Alexander Cruden (Compiled the Cruden's Concordance)

"All other books are of little importance in comparison with the Holy Scriptures."

9. 800 Scientists of Great Britain, recorded in the Bodelian Library, Oxford

"We, the undersigned, students of the natural sciences, desire to express our sincere regret that researches into scientific truth are perverted by some in our own times into occasion for casting doubt into the truth and authenticity of the holy scriptures. We conceive that it is impossible for the Word of God written in the book of nature, and God's Word written in holy scripture, to contradict one another... Physical science is not complete, but is only in a condition of progress. Signed by all 800 scientists."

10. Daniel Webster (US statesman and orator)

"The Bible is the book of faith, and a book of doctrine, and a book of morals, and a book of religion, of special revelation from God; but it is also a book which teaches man his responsibility, his own dignity, and his equality with his fellow man."

"...If we abide by the principles taught in the Bible, our country will go on prospering and to prosper; but if we and our posterity neglect its instructions and authority, no man can bury our glory in profound obscurity." [31]

[32]11. Abraham Lincoln (16th President of the USA)

"In regard to this great book, I have but to say, I believe the Bible is the best gift God has given to man. All the good Saviour gave to the world was communicated through this book. But for this book we could not know right from wrong. All things most desirable for man's welfare, here and hereafter, are to be found portrayed in it."

12. Winston Churchill (British Prime Minister during World War II)

"We rest with assurance upon the impregnable rock of Holy Scripture."

13. General Douglas MacArthur (A US military genius, and general commander of allied forces in SW Pacific during World War II)

" Believe me Sir, never a night goes by, be I ever so tired, but I read the Word of God before I go to bed."

14. John Quincy Adams (6th President of the USA)

"I speak as a man of the world to men of the world; and I say to you, search the scriptures! The Bible is the book of all others, to be read at all ages, and in all conditions of human life; not to be read once or twice or thrice through, and then laid aside but to be read in small portions of one or two chapters everyday, and never to be intermitted, unless by some overruling necessity."

15. Sir Isaac Newton (English philosopher and mathematician; formulator of the law of gravitation)
"We account the scriptures of God to be the most sublime philosophy. I find more sure marks of authority in the Bible than in any profane history whatever."[32]

Let me conclude with the words of **Charles Dickens, the great English novelist and author of "David Copperfield", "Great Expectations" and "Oliver Twist":**

"IT IS THE BEST BOOK THAT EVER WAS OR EVER WILL BE IN THE WORLD!"

REFERENCES

CHAPTER I

1 - 1 Excerpts from *Evidence That Demands A Verdict*, Volume 1, p. 15 1B Josh McDowell Published by Here's Life Publishers, Inc.

CHAPTER 5

2 - 2 Excerpts from *Dake's Annotated reference Bible* Page 509,510

3 - 3Excerpts from *Dake's Annotated reference Bible* Page 509,510

CHAPTER 6

4 - 4 Excerpts from *Evidence That Demands A Verdict*, Volume 1, p. 38 3B 8D Josh McDowell Published by Here's Life Publishers, Inc.

5 - 5 Excerpts from *Evidence That Demands A Verdict*, Volume 1, p. 30 2C 1D Josh McDowell Published by Here's Life Publishers, Inc.

6 - 6 Excerpts from *Evidence That Demands A Verdict*, Volume 1, p. 29-30 2B 1D, 2D Josh McDowell Published by Here's Life Publishers, Inc.

7 - 7 Excerpts from *Evidence That Demands A Verdict*, Volume 1, p. 36 3B 2C Josh McDowell Published by Here's Life Publishers, Inc.

8 - 8 Excerpts from *Evidence That Demands A Verdict,* Volume 1, p. 30 3C 1D Josh McDowell Published by Here's Life Publishers, Inc.

9 - 9 Excerpts from *Evidence That Demands A Verdict*, Volume 1, p. 31 3C 2D Josh McDowell Published by Here's Life Publishers, Inc.

10 - 10 Excerpts from *Evidence That Demands A Verdict*, Volume 1, p. 31 3C 3D Josh McDowell Published by Here's Life Publishers, Inc.

11 - 11 Excerpts from *Evidence That Demands A Verdict*, Volume 1, p. 29 3A 2C Josh McDowell Published by Here's Life Publishers, Inc.

12 - 12 Excerpts from *Evidence That Demands A Verdict*, Volume 1, p. 35-36 4D Josh McDowell Published by Here's Life Publishers, Inc.

13 - 13 Excerpts from Dake's Annotated Reference Bible p. 511 col 1,4

14 - 14 Excerpts from *Evidence That Demands A Verdict*, Volume 1, p. 35-36 4D Josh McDowell Published by Here's Life Publishers, Inc.

CHAPTER 7

15 -15 Excerpts from *Evidence That Demands A Verdict*, Volume 1, p. 33 7C 1D, 2D Josh McDowell Published by Here's Life Publishers, Inc.

16 - 16 Excerpts from *Evidence That Demands A Verdict*, Volume 1, p. 33-35 7C 3D Josh McDowell Published by Here's Life Publishers, Inc.

CHAPTER 9

17 - 17 Excerpts from *Evidence That Demands A Verdict*, Volume 1, p.39 Part 1 4A 1C Josh McDowell Published by Here's Life Publishers, Inc.

18 - 18 Excerpts from *Evidence That Demands A Verdict*, Volume 1, p.19

Part 1 4C 1D, Josh McDowell Published by Here's Life Publishers, Inc.

19 - 19 Excerpts from *Evidence That Demands A Verdict*, Volume 1, p.41,

Part 1 4A 1C Josh McDowell Published by Here's Life Publishers, Inc.

20 - 20 Excerpts from *Evidence That Demands A Verdict*, Volume 1, p.65

Josh McDowell Published by Here's Life Publishers, Inc.

21 - 21 Excerpts from *Evidence That Demands A Verdict*, Volume 1, p.16-17, Section 1 1C Josh McDowell Published by Here's Life Publishers, Inc.

22 - 22 Excerpts from *Evidence That Demands A Verdict*, Volume 1, p.16-17, Section 1 1C Josh McDowell Published by Here's Life Publishers, Inc., Dakes Annotated Reference Bible, Page 241, Col. 3

23- 23 Dakes Annotated Reference Bible, Page 241, Col. 3

24 - 24 Excerpts from *Evidence That Demands A Verdict*, Volume 1, p.18-19, Section 1 2C Josh McDowell Published by Here's Life Publishers, Inc.

25 - 25 Excerpts from *Evidence That Demands A Verdict*, Volume 1, p.19, Section 1 3C Josh McDowell Published by Here's Life Publishers, Inc.

25 - 25 Excerpts from *Evidence That Demands A Verdict*, Volume 1, p.19, Section 1 4C 1D Josh McDowell Published by Here's Life Publishers, Inc.

26 - 26 Excerpts from *Evidence That Demands A Verdict*, Volume 1, p.20, Section 1 4C 2D Josh McDowell Published by Here's Life Publishers, Inc.

27 - 27 Excerpts from *Evidence That Demands A Verdict*, Volume 1, p.21, 4C 3D Josh McDowell Published by Here's Life Publishers, Inc.

28 - 28 Excerpts from *Evidence That Demands A Verdict*, Volume 1, p.22, Section 1 5C 1D Josh McDowell Published by Here's Life Publishers, Inc.

29 - 29 Excerpts from *Evidence That Demands A Verdict*, Volume 1, p.23-24, 6C 3B Josh McDowell Published by Here's Life Publishers, Inc.

CHAPTER I 1

30 - 30 Excerpts from The Power of Faith, Article in October 1999 Issue of Reader's Digest, author, Phyllis McIntosh.

CHAPTER 20

31 - 31 Excerpts from Dake's Annotated Reference Bible p. 243

32-32 Public Domain

Other books by Dag Heward-Mills

Poison: Taming Your Tongue

In this book, Dr Dag Heward-Mills describes the deadly poison found in the tongue, and provides lessons for taming this unruly part of our bodies. Full of real-life stories, this book will minister to you in a practical and interesting way.

The Beast of Prodigality

Are you the head of an ant or the leg of an elephant? How many chances will you have in this life? Why do some people walk away from obviously great opportunities? This vintage teaching examines the syndrome of prodigality.

The Strange Woman

Are you "strange"? What does the Bible mean by "strange woman"? In this revealing book, Bishop Dag Heward-Mills shares with you some vital secrets on how to protect your life and ministry from strange people.

Name it! Claim it! Take it!

In this book, the author shows the believer a *master* key to receiving spiritual, physical, financial and material breakthrough.

They Went to Hell

Does life end in the grave? Is there life after death? These are some of life's great mysteries. Allow Dr Dag Heward-Mills to take you on a journey beyond the grave and find out for yourself what actually exists after death.

Bearing Fruit After Your Own Kind

Do you want to be great in God's kingdom? Do you want to bear much fruit in the Lord? In what areas can God use you? In his usual style, Dag Heward-Mills lucidly expounds the spiritual truth of bearing fruit after your own kind.

Forgiveness Made Easy

Is there any sin that God will not forgive? What is the litmus test for forgiveness? This book is a must for every Christian who desires to walk in unbroken fellowship with God. Leap from pain to joy as Dag Heward-Mills outlines biblical keys to successful relationships.

All About Fornication

What are the complications of fornication? Are you insulated from this sin? Discover more about the international and cross-cultural sin of fornication in this book. Dag Heward-Mills presents the reader with practical steps on how to climb out and stay out of the pit of fornication!

Frugality

This book is phenomenal! Is your business improving? Is your church growing? What does it mean to have a big front door and a big back door? How can I prosper in good times and in bad times? Enjoy the practical and down to earth teaching in this book.

The Minister's Handbook

This book is a compilation of the material a minister needs to conduct various ceremonies such as marriages, funerals, baptisms   naming ceremonies, etc. It has been presented in an easy-to-use format which all pastors will find very helpful.

Anagkazo: Compelling Power

Learn about this "compelling power" which makes evangelism effective and fruitful even in the face of opposition, excuse, suspicion, resentment, etc. This book by Dag Heward-Mills can make you more of a soul-winner than you have ever been!

The Mega Church

The heart cry of God is for the world to be saved, and for His house - the church - to be filled! From this revelation was born this book by Bishop Dag Heward-Mills.

Backsliding: Develop Your Staying Power

Though an unusual subject, "backsliding" deals with a very common occurrence among Christians. Many begin, but not so many survive to the end. In this book, Bishop Dag Heward-Mills sounds the alarm, and graphically shows why every Christian must make it to heaven!

Beauty

What do you know about beauty? Is beauty one of the things you are looking for in a wife? Be enlightened as Dag Heward-Mills carefully and systematically outlines the ten attributes of physical beauty in this book.

Born Again

What does it mean to be "born again"? What is not the same as being born again? Will I go to heaven if I'm not born again? In this interesting book, Dag Heward-Mills throws more light on many of the misconceptions about the "born again" experience!

Duality

Are people really straight forward? Have you ever met someone who seems to have two personalities? Meet the perfect pretender in Brother Dag Heward-Mills' classic exposé on the double personality. This timeless message is a must for every sincere believer.

Ministerial Ethics

In this outstanding work, Brother Dag Heward-Mills examines real-life situations in ministry today. He addresses practical issues like finances, politics and ministerial interactions. This book is a must for every Christian leader.

Principles of Success

Only one man in the Bible is described as "a man after God's heart." What earned him this reputation? Are the principles that made him successful in the eyes of both God and man relevant to the believer today? Find out in this exciting book!

Supernatural Power

A lot of mysteries surround the spiritual realm, no doubt. But the fact still stands that the "supernatural" is real! Join Bishop Dag Heward-Mills in this exciting trip to the world of the supernatural and discover how to access this realm!

One Hundred Percent Answered Prayer

You prayed for something and didn't get it... Out of the frustration and the disappointment, you quit praying... Familiar isn't it? The question then is: can one experience one hundred percent results to prayer? Yes, yes, YES! Find out how!

Unbeatable Prosperity

The ability to prosper comes from God, and it is His will for the believer to experience unbeatable prosperity! As you read this book, let faith and confidence be stirred up in you, and lead you to possess your possessions!

Strategies for Prayer

Knowing what to pray for and how to pray make prayer enjoyable. In this excellent book, Bishop Dag Heward-Mills reveals certain strategies for prayer which will revitalise your prayer life, and give you a sense of direction.

Catch the Anointing

This exceptional book by Bishop Dag Heward-Mills will teach you what it means to "catch the anointing" and how you can be anointed for ministry. Learn how to catch the anointing for the work of ministry. This book is a must for every minister.

Lay People and the Ministry

Based on his experience of the lay ministry, Dag Heward-Mills shows why the Great Commission cannot be fulfilled without this biblical concept of lay people getting involved in the work. Learn how to combine your secular profession with real and effective ministry.

Solomonic Success

Learn about Solomon's success in this enlightening book, the third in the success series by Bishop Dag Heward-Mills.

Secrets of Success

All through the Scriptures, God has made it abundantly clear that success is included in His master plan for the believer's life here on earth. But how can one experience biblical and real success? This book gives the answer to that question.

7 Great Principles

At last this popular and powerful teaching is on the printed page! Seven Great Principles will enlighten you about the effect of salvation on the spirit, soul and body of a person. May God grant you the spirit of wisdom and revelation as you read this book!

Leaders and Loyalty

Some are born leaders. Some develop into leaders. In this classic book, Bishop Dag Heward-Mills teaches on how this ingredient of loyalty consolidates a leader's performance. Using biblical, historic and literary references, the subject is made even more relevant to every kind of leader.

Transform Your Pastoral Ministry

In an era when there are not so many pastoral success stories this is indeed a welcome book. Bishop Dag Heward-Mills, a very successful pastor himself, explains why and how it is possible to make the pastoral ministry effective.

Loyalty and Disloyalty (Hardback book)

Though a primary requirement of God for leaders, very little has been written on this subject. In this book, Dag Heward-Mills outlines very important principles with the intention of increasing the stability of churches. So relevant and practical is the content of this book that it has become an indispensable tool for many church leaders.

Win the Lost At Any Cost

I have become all things to all men so that by all means I might save some (1 Corinthians 9:22). These words by the Apostle Paul reflect the heart of a soul winner: to win the lost at any cost! In this thought-provoking book, Dag Heward-Mills seeks to stir up all believers to the urgency of the task of saving the lost, for the end of the age is at hand!

The Art of Leadership

The call to ministry is a call to leadership. Once again with a casual and down-to-earth approach, Dr. Heward-Mills expounds on principles that have made him an outstanding Christian leader. The truths revealed here will inspire many to the art of leadership.

For additional information on Dag Heward-Mills' books, tapes and videos write to these addresses:

In Africa:

Parchment House,

P .O. Box 114 Korle-Bu,

Accra Ghana

West Africa

Rest of the world:

Lighthouse Chapel International

PO. Box 3706

London NW2 1YJ

United Kingdom

Website:

www.lighthousechapel.org

About The Author

Dag Heward-Mills, a medical doctor by profession, is a minister of the Gospel who has been used by the Lord in healing crusades worldwide. Dubbed 'Healing Jesus Crusades', these meetings usually attract several thousand people.

Many notable miracles have accompanied Dr. Heward-Mills' Healing Jesus Crusades. These phenomenal miracles, attested to by medical doctors, have included the opening of the eyes of the blind, the restoring of hearing to the deaf, the emptying of wheel chairs and even the raising of the dead.

Indeed, some of the authentic supernatural occurrences that have been documented in this doctor-turned-preacher's healing meetings defy medical science. Perhaps the most spectacular of these events which confirms the Scripture in Acts 2:22, '...a man approved of God among you by miracles and wonders and signs,' is the appearance of the glory of God in a halo over a crusade tent, in one of his mass healing campaigns.

Bishop Dag Heward-Mills is the Bishop and Founder of the Lighthouse Chapel International, a charismatic denomination with over 400 branches in the United States, Europe, Africa, Asia and Australia. He is a member of Dr. David Yonggi Cho's Church Growth International Board.

Bishop Heward-Mills lives in Accra with his wife Adelaide and their four children.